CHARLESTON DOGS

CHARLESTON DOGS

LUCY SPECTOR
EDITOR

FREDERIC C. BEIL

SAVANNAH

TO

OUR AGENCIES

Animal Rescue & Relief
John Ancrum Society for the Prevention of
Cruelty to Animals
Pet Helpers Rescue and Adoption Shelter

AND OUR
DOCTORS OF VETERINARY MEDICINE

Lara Allison
Eve M. Badger
J. Todd Baker
Ann M. Beck
Katherine J. Benton
Todd Benton
Douglas Berger
John Biascoechea
Dan Bieck
Michelle Bilger
Linnea Bredenberg
Patrick T. Breen
Anne F. Briley
R. Keith Bryan
Kim Carroll
Andrea Cavedo
Allison Chappell
Cynthia Goodstein Cleland
Holley Cone
Jessica Cote

v

DEDICATION

Lauren H. Crymes
Nancy Dangerfield
Dennis A. Feinberg
Lynne M. Flood
Michael Forcier
Kim Fortney
Gerald W. George
Thomas J. Hentges
Christopher M. Hill
Thomas A. Hutto, Jr.
Merrill P. Irvin
Tracy Jagocki
Abigail Kaufman
Paul Kerwin
Brian King
Sally Brown Lanford
Lynda T. Leffler
Bridget E. Luke
R. Mitchell McCullers
Jean M. McKee
Bruce Mackinnon
Martha McTavish
Carmela Malark
Michelle Mayers
Katherine L. Momeier
John D. Ohlandt, Jr.
Paul D. Patrick III
Robert T. Pernell
Jean Pitcairn
Christopher R. Powers
Chad Reynolds
Ruth M. Roberts
Michelle Rockwell

DEDICATION

Billy Roumillat
Katherine A. Saenger
Scott G. Senf
Calley C. Sharon
Paul M. Shealy
Thomas J. Sheridan
Janathan Shong
Laura Shuler
Cynthia P. Smith
Harry Smith
James H. Southard
Karen Spencer
David E. Steele
Mindy R. Stelling
Otto M. Strock
Susan B. Thompson
Lauren C. Tierney
Wendy Whitlock
Wilbur L. Wise

Recollect that the Almighty,
who gave the dog to be companion
of our pleasures and our toils,
hath invested him with
a nature noble and incapable of deceit.

—Sir Walter Scott, *The Talisman*

CONTENTS

Editor's Note   xv

Baemours Faithful Star   1

Rocco Jones   4

Quail Run's Carolina Hoppin John   6

Sunny Moore   9

Dunelm Maidavale Blue Poppy   12

Edward Legaré Likes   14

Max Browder   16

Bohicket Semmes   18

Peyton Simpson   21

Jessie Mae   24

Ballou   26

Sophie Tucker   28

Brix Cummings   30

Andy and Kiwi Bunting   32

Lady   34

Valiant   37

Rosie   40

Cricket Noel II   44

Poogan   46

Darby Bartko   48

Samantha Bernstein   50

Rufus   52

Charlie Burbage   54

Rob Roy MacGregor   56

Sirius the Dog Star   59

Sadie Greenberg   62

Bella Gabriella of Charleston   63

CONTENTS

Athens   65

Red   67

Benjamin   69

Lucky   72

Lady Hancock   76

Charleston Dogs   79

Buckshot's Little Griffin   83

Lucky   86

Buckshot Faith   89

I'm Just Wild About Harry   92

St. James Electric Slide   94

Edisto Herring   96

The Little White Dog   99

Samantha   101

Louis Armstrong   104

Tann Mann   107

Cleo and Fletcher Kammeyer   110

Bea Waring   112

Spensir Quillinan   115

Scout Ross   117

Xzena   119

Ellie   121

Maximilian   122

Gracie Peters   124

Danny Dog   126

Admiral Lord Nelson V   128

Boo-Boo   130

Tashi and Chai   133

Dolly   136

Jose   138

CONTENTS

Otis and Shasta   141

Mr. Emmett   144

Z   146

Lily Sommons   149

Libby Lou Singer   151

Saxon   153

Summer   155

CeeDee   157

Magdala Rose   161

Piper   163

Tippa Sullivan Wood   165

Chelsea   168

Bob   171

Dundalk He's a Lover   173

Lion Lee Waitzman   175

Covington's Surfer Boy   177

Fuzzy Prozac Turner   179

Sedgewick Emmerton Torrence   182

Alexa Tomlin   185

Nemo Wannamaker   188

Lily   190

Gizmo Settle   193

Tiffany   196

Camilla   199

Sera   201

Higgins   203

Piebald   207

Lizzy   208

Sadie   211

Jiggs Campbell   213

CONTENTS

Katie Scarlett   215
Rhett   218
Dracula   222
Diamond   224
Foxy and Sassy   226
Hazel and Shiloh   228
Rockem Sockem Roo   231
Zoey   233

EDITOR'S NOTE

As the editor of *Charleston Dogs,* I am moved with both humor and hope by this collection of dog tales. My wish is that the "human pack" will understand, as our various breeds do, that "we dogs" in every way are blessed to share this holy city with our two-legged companions. As your stories and biographies arrived on my desk at the Dog Art Dealer gallery, I wagged my tail and barked with glee and gratitude while reading your unique stories.

As an English cocker spaniel, I cherish my kinship with Charleston's animals and humans. I am a firm believer in the spiritual importance of a dog's presence in humans' lives. Hopefully our humans will learn from these Charleston dogs more about how to live life, with our enthusiasm and honesty every moment every day.

Edward Hoagland in *Dogs and the Tug of Life* suggests: "In order to really enjoy a dog, one doesn't merely try to train him to be semi-human. The point of it is to open oneself to the possibility of becoming partly dog."

Thank you for your efforts to make this such an entertaining book. This book is dedicated to the organizations and veterinarians who provide assistance to dogs-in-need in our city and to the sacrifices made by those in all communities to save and shelter many of my lost and bewildered friends during hurricane Katrina. My acknowledgment and gratitude is extended to them all.

Sincerely,

LUCY SPECTOR

CHARLESTON DOGS

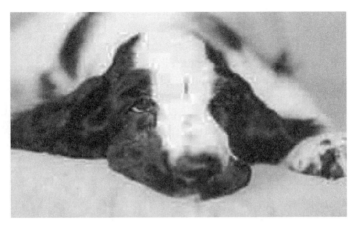

BAEMOURS FAITHFUL STAR
("ABIGAIL WILLIAMS," "ABBY")

I was born in Owings Mill, Maryland, but came to Charleston when I was nine months old. My dad is the rector of St. Stephen's Episcopal Church in Ansonborough, and my mom is an interior designer.

But let me tell you about being a dog in Charleston. It's been great fun, but at first I was perplexed. There were these huge "dogs" that had long tails, made a clopping sound when they came up the street, and they pulled wagons. I would bark to them, but they didn't bark back. As dogs often do, I wanted to get closer for, well, you know, a sniff. But they were way too tall for that, and, besides, there was that huge tail. After a while we just got used to each other, but Dad told me finally that they were not dogs at all.

The other things I love about Charleston are palmetto bugs, although back where I'm from we called them cockroaches. My cat sister, Corky, and I like to

1

play "palmetto bug hockey," where she and I try to bounce them around our patio and score points against each other.

Then there's Folly Beach and the Isle of Palms. Being an English cocker spaniel, I just love the beach, so Dad takes me there on a long leash and I get to swim in the warm water during the summer.

Charleston is what my dad calls a "nasal nirvana." Jasmine, and tea olives, and the flowers of spring and summer—all of this is wonderful for me. That's why I love to walk all over town. Everywhere you go there is something new to smell, and the closer I get to the restaurants on Meeting Street, the more excited I get. Actually I'm on the prowl for chicken bones that any savvy dog can find in the bushes around town. When I get ahold of one, my mother screams bloody murder. I can't tell you how hard it is to hide a bone in your mouth. Nonchalance is not one of my strong suits, although I'm learning.

Then there is the church. One of the great things about churches with balconies is that you can run up the stairs and see the world from a whole new perspective. Dogs spend most of their lives looking straight ahead or up. From the balcony, I can put my head through those spokes and look down on everyone.

This year we had a Blessing of the Animals, the day when we remember St. Francis of Assisi, the patron saint of animals. There were so many dogs that I lost count, and there were even two miniature horses from one of the carriage companies. After it was all over, there were so many smells in the yard that it took a whole week before I had done a complete "inventory."

Charleston is my home now, and all the beaches are my summer playgrounds. I am now *Canis familia-*

ris charlestoniana—"by choice" (Dad told me to write that).

And I can't tell you how much I love this town—tea olives, jasmine, horses, chicken bones, and all!

ABBY

ROCCO JONES
("LITTLE MAN")

For everyone there are those days when the world seems too large for one small person to face. When those days come, and they always do, I put on an old Frank Sinatra album and I look at my dog.

When Ole Blue Eyes begins to croon, "Just what makes that little old ant think he can move that rubber tree plant? Everyone knows an ant can't move a rubber tree plant," the inspiration to conquer the big, bad world begins to surge through my veins.

So where does the dog fit in, you ask?

Well, my dog, Rocco, is the living embodiment of that ant. My little man has definitely got "high apple pie in the sky hopes."

From being the runt of the litter, so fragile he had to be given mouth-to-mouth resuscitation at birth in order to keep life in his tiny frame, Rocco has become a Lilliputian soldier overcoming Gulliver on his travels, a diminutive Mayan tearing through the jungles of Mexico, a little Napoleon claiming foreign lands.

Think for a moment of going through life weighing a mere three and a half pounds. Everything Rocco encounters is, for him, of gigantic proportions. But like a little David, he conquers the Goliaths of the world head on.

He stands up to Rottweilers, tomcats, fire hydrants standing an intimidating two feet tall, and the occasional ankle of our mail delivery person. All this and more, with his head held high, his chest puffed out, and a look of unwavering confidence in his solid stare.

But at the end of the day Rocco is still my dog, curled in my lap, sleepy and satisfied after a long, hard day of conquering that big, bad world.

Sure, he may seem like just a dog to you, albeit a very cute dog, but to me he is a constant reminder that even the smallest creatures in this vast world in which we live can make an enormous difference.

So my advice to you the next time you're "found with your chin on the ground," is to look toward your little inspiration, be it dog, cat, bird, or rat, remember that valiant ant, hold up your head and puff out your chest, and yell to the world at the top of your voice . . .

"Oops, there goes another rubber tree plant!"

JAMY GREY JONES

QUAIL RUN'S
CAROLINA HOPPIN JOHN
("RAFTER")

My Australian shepherd, Rafter, was named for the now retired Australian tennis star, Patrick Rafter. Both were born to large litters, Rafter (eight) and Patrick (nine). Patrick donated a large part of his U.S. Open winnings to a children's hospital; Rafter loves kids and visits two children's hospitals (MUSC and MCG) as a therapy dog. Both are very good looking and exude personality!

Rafter was born in Lady Lake, Florida, a New Year's Day baby. As a youngster he was introduced to many activities: competitive obedience, agility, sheep herding, and pet therapy. He loved everything and participated in each with characteristic exuberance. Soon I found out that he was destined for a special mission.

At two he was diagnosed with osteosarcoma, a type of bone cancer. I was devastated to learn that his only hope for another six to nine months of life was radiation therapy. I decided to give him the chance, so each Monday, Wednesday, and Friday for the next four weeks, we drove to the University of Georgia in Athens, where he received his treatments. He handled them well and especially liked the tradition of stopping at Wendy's on the drive home for a grilled chicken sandwich. He awoke from the anesthesia just enough to eat and then promptly passed out till we got home, where he was ready for dinner! At the start of Rafter's treatment we had been warned that he would lose weight. By the end of his ordeal, however, he had gained four pounds! I began to cook healthy meals for him. I also added supplements to his diet and spent every minute I could just being with him. That was almost three years ago. His cervical vertebra has regenerated healthy bone tissue, and now Rafter is the picture of health!

Although we had to discontinue agility, sheep herding, and obedience because of the jumping involved, therapy has brought out his natural talent as a performer and entertainer. He visits several local nursing homes, schools, and MUSC and MCG, where he makes everyone smile with his tricks. Our home visits to a young boy being treated for brain cancer inspired the beginning of a new program called the K-9 Care Unit for Kids. There are about twenty therapy teams who are available for free home visits to children fighting chronic illnesses. The dogs take the children's minds off their medical problems and make them feel better.

Rafter is known among friends as "a character." I began taking him to the vet's office every two or three weeks to weigh him, and gave him cookies afterward. Now as soon as we pull into the parking lot he shrieks with excitement and is the only dog in the waiting room that whines and pulls to get into the exam room! His nickname there is the "Cookie Monster."

Rafter's affinity for food has created my most entertaining memories. One year at a Christmas party for a

Mt. Pleasant nursing home, Rafter was doing a trick where he pulls his friend Peaches the Pomeranian in a little red wagon. The towel he was pulling her with came untied. As I went over to retie it, I looked over my shoulder and saw my well-trained dog stand up on his hind legs and snatch a tree off their gingerbread-house display! At least he didn't take the whole house!

There was also the time at Thanksgiving I caught him in the dining room, standing on his hind legs, and licking the butter. Again he was considerate and didn't eat the whole thing. Once I turned it over, no one could tell anyway!

Fortunately my family loves Rafter. Once, when my mother and aunt were visiting for lunch, I added some of his freshly cooked chicken to our soup. As we were eating, my mother commented, "I remember the days when the dog got the leftovers!"

It's probably a good thing that our agility career was cut short. One year at the Pet Fest he was doing an agility demo and jumped the fence in the middle of the course, ran over to beg a cookie from a bystander, then jumped back in, and finished!

I, too, am a cancer survivor, and have learned from Rafter to tackle each day with excitement and happiness, never to take a moment with loved ones for granted, and to enjoy as many cookies as we can get!

JANE HIRSCH

SUNNY MOORE ("SUNNO")

Getting lost is a very scary thing, worse when you are a puppy, still pretty bad when grown up.

The first time I wandered off I was five months old. How well I remember it. Tall grass, people calling me, whistling, generally panicked. Emerging from the grass, I immediately fell into a small stream. My family showed up pronto to rescue me. Wet, terrified, and happy, I vowed never to get lost again.

And I didn't—until eleven years later—and what an adventure it was!

One day I was invited to go to a car show, a twenty-minute car ride from home. We walked around the show, and as we passed a hot dog stand a clumsy gentleman dropped his paper tray and I lunged forward, slipped my loosely attached collar, grabbed a hot dog, and ran. Everyone in sight chased me, but I had a good head start and jumped unseen into the back of an antigue truck. I lay down and enjoyed the hot dog.

I must have dozed off as the next thing I knew the truck was underway for points unknown. We arrived at a barn, and once I was alone I snuck out and immediately encountered a large, but friendly looking, goat who introduced himself as Freddy.

"What are you doing here my little friend?" he said.

"I'm lost and heading home," I said.

"And where might that be?" he asked.

And then it hit me. I was, for the second time in my life, really lost. I didn't have a clue where my home was except that it was on a river and the sun set over the far river bank.

"If you live on the river toward the big mountain, you had better go left on the road over there and talk to Agnes, the Jersey cow at the next farm. She is pretty smart." I did as he suggested, and while I walked beside the road I wondered how on earth Lassie had found her way home.

It was starting to get dark when I finally found Agnes. "Good evening, Madam. I don't suppose you know where Plainfield is, do you?"

"I think it's a few miles up this road. My vet lives there," she said with a smile. "Are you lost?" I had to admit that I was.

"I suggest you stay on this road, and when you come to a big oak tree, look for Louis the Owl. He flies over that way and might help you."

I came to a big oak and called out, "Oh, wise old owl, please help me find my home in Plainfield."

Out from the leaves came, "I'm not home, please leave a message."

I wasn't put off by this and said, "If you get me home I'll let you spend the winter in our warm barn, safe from the snow."

He moved out onto the end of a limb and said, "Not a bad trade, my little dog friend. Let's get going before night falls."

So Louis flew overhead guiding me, and I ran along until I thought my little legs would collapse. After we finally made it to the old farmhouse where I lived, I showed Louis the barn, which he liked a lot.

I got a rousing welcome with lots of hugs and treats. I wish I could have told my family about the goat, the cow, and Louis the Owl. My adventure was over, and I vowed never to get lost again.

SUNNO

DUNELM MAIDAVALE
BLUE POPPY
("POPPY")

My life began twelve years ago on two hundred acres in the rolling plains of Middleburg, Virginia, where I spent my first year and a half. Then one afternoon a pretty lady drove through the gates and around to my fence. She approached me and my friends, calling my name. How could she know my name? I wondered. It was love at first sight for us both. After a bath and a haircut, she whisked me away to begin the adventure of my very pampered life.

This lady and I lived a very nice life together, with lots of quiet evenings by the fire, but we always knew something was missing. One afternoon we had a visitor. He began coming more and more, and then he and my mom were married, making us a happy family. We moved into a new house with a beautiful garden where we spent many afternoons on a chaise by the pool. I thought then, How could life be any better? Then one day empty boxes arrived and then a big truck. Mom and Dad were very excited as they knew we were beginning another adventure. The afternoon we left Virginia it was cold and rainy. I climbed into Mom's car and went to sleep. When I awoke, we were in a paradise of balmy breezes and swaying palm trees. We had arrived in Charleston!

I quickly adjusted to life in the Deep South—walks on the Battery, weekends at the beach and sitting on this porch they kept calling a piazza. Soon I made lots of new friends, and now everyone calls me "Miss Poppy." I couldn't be happier than I am in Charleston. The summers can be a little hot, but we take earlier walks and rest during the day. Dog parks, walks on the beach, swimming in the ocean, and evenings with friends on the piazza—life is good!

This past October I celebrated my twelfth birthday. My parents gave me a party, and several of my friends were invited, including Adam Cathcart, my favorite gentleman-caller who is a handsome black Labrador from Church Street. My dear friends Lucy Lee and Khaki Dawson came together, and even my new friend Heidi Crawford from just down the street joined in the festivities. My best girlfriend, Daisy Von Werssowetz, arrived and soon was flitting everywhere (you know what busybodies Jack Russells can be, but I do love her so). Walter Bowers, my tennis court buddy, was there after being freshly groomed and looking ever so handsome. My newest friend is Spensir, the most beautiful blonde Labrador you have ever seen. I think he has a crush on me, and was very upset when Adam arrived. I guess putting two beaus in the same room (piazza) can be a bit much, but my dance card certainly was full!

As I sit on my piazza listening to the gentle breezes and the sound of horses pulling carriages of visitors around our beautiful city, I think that life in Charleston certainly is good!

POPPY

EDWARD LEGARÉ LIKES ("LEGARÉ")

It was a warm August morning at my master's fishing cabin on French Quarter Creek near Cainhoy. My master was reading his book in the front yard. I was doing what I do best—sniffing around. I went to the water's edge in the boat slip to check out what looked like a log. It moved toward me. I barked and next thing I saw was a big mouth and a lot of teeth. It was a gator! His teeth scraped across my face and, trying to pull me into the water, bit down on my big ear. I yelped!

My master jumped up and ran to the slip to see what was splashing. It was me and the gator. My master stepped (barefoot!) on the back of the gator and started stomping on the big gator's snout. The gator let go of me, and I hightailed it into the yard as fast as my little legs would go.

I watched my master stomp a couple of more times on the big gator's nose, not knowing that his foot had somehow managed to get in the gator's mouth. My master got away and we headed for the ER. He ended up with twenty-plus stitches and then three days in the hospital on IV antibiotics after his foot got infected.

Needless to say, I was traumatized some, but have managed to get back to my old basset self.

Pets are lucky to have brave and resourceful masters. We are truly bonded in a special way now—my master and me!

LEGARÉ

MAX
BROWDER

On the morning of December 23, 2003, I, Max, graced the world with my presence. Along for the ride were my two sisters and two brothers. Their names are—well, actually, I do not know there names—but I do remember how much fun they were to wrestle and play fetch with. My mother is a six-pound Yorkshire terrier with unbelievable good looks, and my father is a three-pound Yorkshire terrier with even better looks. I know what you are probably thinking, and, yes, the whole weight thing is a little bazaar, but they really wanted to pass their beauty down to the next generation. So, attention, all beautiful canines, you might want to use this to your advantage (more walks, treats, fetch, etc.)—just droop those beautiful eyeball things and look pitiful, it works every time.

My time was being filled with eating, sleeping, pooping, and, did I mention, sleeping? Now please do not get me wrong. All of those things are wonderful, but it was time for a change. I hinted my eagerness for adventure to my birth mother, and she started to cry. Luckily by the next afternoon all of my jumping around had paid off. In no time my mother was making appointments for me. I could not believe the turnout, that all of these tall nice people were competing to take me on adventures. That afternoon I chose my new mom and tour guide, and I have not looked back since.

It was February 13, 2004, when my adventure began. My mom had to work, so my substitute tour guide, "Grandma," picked me up. Grandma and I drove over the East Cooper bridge into Mt. Pleasant with eagerness and excitement. It was just how I had imagined it would be—treats and kisses in every direction. I could not have taken a wrong turn if I had tried to. Finally my new mom showed up and, boy, was she excited. Sarah carries me around in a satchel from the Discovery Channel store on King Street. She states often, "This is absolutely my best shopping purchase ever!" Sarah also says that about my seat-belt harness from Palmetto Paws, and my collar's by Coach. I had better move on before my dad goes into shock again. Overall, I believe my family is the best present ever from God to me.

My favorite and most fun-filled days are digging in my backyard for fiddler crabs (carefully not letting my mom or dad see me), basking in the sun, flirting with my neighbors, or swimming in the ocean. Oh, I almost forgot, driving to Sullivan Island for a brisk walk is always fun. I just wish we could go before 6 P.M., then my mom and dad would have the energy to run as long as I can. I must wrap this up by thanking my family and my loving veterinarian, Dr. Laura Shuler, for the opportunity to run, jump, and slobber, and to the city of Charleston, South Carolina, for having the best downtown parks a canine could ever explore.

MAX

BOHICKET
SEMMES
("BO")

There is a type of dog on the Charleston Sea Islands that is so distinctive-looking and prolific as to be almost a breed. Johns Island Ditch Dogs, Wadmalaw Black Dogs, these dogs are dark-colored, some hound-like, others more like Labs. They all have white, wing-like markings on their chests and white hairs on one or more feet. I think that these dogs are as close to an indigenous species on these islands as the Dingo is in Australia.

One freezing November morning in 1995, I came across such a dog, a tiny puppy standing in the middle of Bohicket Road. As anyone who has ever rescued a dog from the side of the road knows, the actual process is generally, mercifully, a blur. I remember jumping barefoot from my car, flagging down oncoming trucks, and, after a short chase into a bracken-filled ditch, scooping up an emaciated, half-dead puppy.

I named him Bohicket after the road he survived. He was feral, yet not fearful of people, and I believe that in his short life he had never known a human at all. But he knew crows—mortal enemies then and now. My veterinarian pronounced him good Johns Island stock—a Darwinian marvel—probably the first in his lineage to

18

live in a house and, no doubt, the first to sleep in a bed. Prognosis for domestication—poor.

I had been mother to two golden retrievers, but I soon discovered that a hound is not a Golden and a Johns Island Ditch Dog is not a normal hound. The raising of Bohicket was more of a challenge than I could have ever imagined. Complex and willful, intelligent and exuberant, he grew to be ninety pounds—all legs—and single-minded in his need to *chase*. Walking Bohicket on a leash was much like water skiing without the water, but often with the inevitable wipeout. Housebreaking was not a possibility.

In time even the worst nightmares fade, and now, years later, those memories are sweetly tempered. I gaze fondly at the chewed woodwork we couldn't bear to sand smooth, a sight as endearing as baby's teethmarks on a bottle. I smile when I recall the massive, teetering pile of stained rugs, chewed shoes and clothes, and the demolished couch, the monument to Bohicket's puppyhood, destined to remain for eons in the Charleston landfill.

In his tenth year Bohicket is still high-strung and dubiously housebroken, but he has finally settled somewhat. Grey-muzzled and still physically graceful, he has a quirky, dry sense of humor, and age has endowed him with a dignified air. He is the star of parties, yet sometimes there is separateness, a brooding pensiveness about him that inspired my daughter to call him "The Edgar Allan Poe of Dogs." He completely loves us, his human pack members, and welcomes cuddling, though he rarely licks. He is also my muse and, as a painter of dogs, I have painted him often. In Low Country landscapes, his attenuated silhouette is almost cartoon like—the universal sign for hound dog. But he is best in portraits—silly and surprised in a field of flowers or reclining, Roman-nosed and regal, against a silk cushion. He is a marvelous dog; proof that there are no lost causes in the dog world. When I think of how far we've come together since those frustrating early days, I'm reminded of the saying: 'That which comes too easily we esteem too lightly." How true.

FAITH CAMERON SEMMES

PEYTON SIMPSON ("PEYT")

Peyton was found in a puppy mill in Upstate, South Carolina. The conditions in the puppy mill were devastating for her. She was born in a barn and lived there with around two hundred other dogs for a little over a year, before she was rescued. The barn was very dark at all times with no windows. She stayed in a small rabbit hutch, where she had no human contact whatsoever. She was fed scarcely and would have to eat her own feces just to stay alive. While at this puppy mill, she had never gone outside the barn, she had never seen daylight or even grass. By the time she was rescued, she was found with ulcers in her eyes from where the wire from the hutch had stabbed her in the eyes, and she was never taken to a vet for medication. As a matter of fact, she had never seen a vet from the time she was born up until that time.

Once she was rescued, she was taken to the Charleston Animal Rescue and Relief. She was immediately taken to the vet to get all her shots and to find out what problems she may have had, as well as receive medication for her eyes. The doctor reported she had a low heart rate, some problems with her teeth, as well as luxating patellas. She had to receive all of her shots that she had never received and needed up to this point.

At the Animal Rescue and Relief here in Charleston they have taught her so many things and been so good to her. She learned how to simply walk and play in the grass. She is now housebroken. Peyton would go to the bathroom on herself when she saw humans because she had never been around humans whatsoever, so she had to learn how to adjust. At the house with the Rescue and Relief they had to use a night light for light because Peyton was so used to the dark in the barn. She couldn't handle normal sunlight or lamps, as they were too bright for her. She also learned how to walk up and down stairs, as she had never even seen stairs before. Peyton was still very skittish of new people, but was very friendly to the ones she new from the Rescue.

The first time I saw Peyton was on the Animal Rescue and Relief website. My hope was that she would like us as much as we liked her. The director, Michelle Reid, had contacted me and told me they could bring Peyton for a home visit and see how we liked her or, more importantly, how she would react to us. My husband, Bobby, and I both fell in love with her right away. She was very frightened of both of us during that first visit. Michelle told us that we could keep her over a weekend to see how she would react to us. After we kept her for several days, we could tell a huge difference after she got to know us. So we officially adopted her.

Peyton is doing great with us now. She is still scared when she meets new people. She is named after Peyton Manning, who played football for Tennessee. She loves to watch Tennessee play football. We would like to thank Michelle and the Animal Rescue and Relief for allowing us to adopt Peyton. She is a great asset to our family.

BOBBY AND SUMMAR SIMPSON

JESSIE MAE

Jessie is my name, and hunting is my game. I am one of those "hard-headed, fun-loving, never-stops" Jack Russell terriers. I love it here in Charleston. Born and bred here and never leaving. I love chasing seagulls on the beach. I love boating down the Edisto. I love chasing squirrels in my backyard. I love running and barking at what my momma says is "nothing." She is silly because there is always something to bark at! I have even learned to howl like a hound dog, and do it several times a day whenever the train goes by. Yep, I am definitely a Charleston dog.

I used to take my family, food, house, yard, and other dog friends for granted. One day I was so busy hunting that I did not notice my dog collar going off. I kept digging under the fence and got out into the wide big world, and into the swampy forest behind our acres of fenced space. I can tell you right now that I do *not* take any of this for granted anymore. For one full week I was more scared than I ever care to admit—being a Jack Russell and all.

I ended up down the road and some lady picked me up. She took me in her truck about eight miles up the road from where I live. I think she was gonna keep me, because she put food and water out, but I did not get to sleep in the bed. There was a mean man who lived with her and who kicked me and was mean to me.

Thank goodness for my real momma. She never gave up on me. She got together a posse of her friends, posted pictures of me everywhere, went on TV, called the radio stations—well, she never quit looking. One evening a very kind man called her and said, "I know where your dog is." And I think that it probably only took her five seconds to get to me. She knocked on the door of the place where I was being fed and entered the house. When she opened the door to leave, I literally fell into the house. I was tired, hungry, dirty, and bruised. She was tired and had gone for many nights without sleep just looking for me. We hugged and hugged and cried together. It was the best moment of my life. I wish that all dogs could have a momma like her—she never gave up. And you can bet that when I hear my collar go off and I am digging by the fence that I will *never* go out of my yard again, unless it is a very good catch! After all, I am a Jack Russell terrier!

JESSIE

BALLOU

Have you ever looked up to the heavens and wondered if there really are angels among us? My name is Ballou, I'm a Leonberger, and I'm here to tell you angels do exist.

My story starts on a sad note. Somehow I was stolen from a litter of pups on Johns Island. My human mother, Tracey, once told me that I was dropped from a truck onto Folly Road, where a kind person rescued me and took me to Pet Helpers. Everyone knew I would be adopted, but it was very late on a Saturday, and the humans were ready to go home.

I was hiding under a chair when my very first angel arrived. Tyler was ten years old, and when she hugged me it felt like I was home. She kissed me, and told me I was safe and not to be afraid. Tyler's mom, Tracey, agreed to foster me for the weekend. But then my soon-to-be human dad, Steve, saw us together and knew we were all meant to be a family.

At their (my) house I met two more angels disguised as little girls. Grayson, who was six, cried with such love and happiness over me that all I could do was to keep licking her face. I still think she is the sweetest tasting thing that has ever been created. My other angel, two-year-old Olivia, became my new littermate. Together we learned to run, nap, eat, and give loads of unconditional love.

I had massive paws and looked like a bear, so I was named Ballou, like the Jungle Book bear. Life was fabulous. Then one morning I woke up so sick that I couldn't lift my head. The culprit was Parvo Virus—a nasty strain—and all I remember as I lay in Dr. Ohlandt's Veterinary Hospital was dreaming about my three little girl-angels and how much I missed them. After many days I heard Dr. Bilger on the phone telling my mom that she thought I might be giving up, that I might not make it through the day.

My human mom's a fighter, and the next thing I remember, she was crawling into my cage. She hugged me and said there were three little souls at home who needed me to protect them while we grew up.

That's when Heaven touched down here on Earth. My mother gently put something tenderly under my nose. That's when I smelled the scent that can still put me on Cloud Nine. I smelled my three girls, my angels. Mom had brought the pajamas they'd worn that night. I knew, instantly, it was my responsibility to get better and take care of my girls. I was only four months old, but I knew the truth right then.

Today I am two years old, forty inches tall, and 145 pounds! I am beyond grateful for the love and kindness of my family, who never gave up on each other. Everyone who sees me says, "Wow, that's a big dog! What kind of a dog is that?" I just smile, wag my tail, and think, "These are my angels, Tyler, Grayson, and Olivia, and I am Ballou, their faithful Leonberger."

BALLOU ERWIN

SOPHIE TUCKER ("SOPHIE")

You might say I'm the new terrier in town. I moved from Connecticut to Charleston in December with my parents, Janice and Michael. Even with my fur I wasn't fond of the cold weather up North, but an occasional frolic in the snow was fun.

At the tender age of six months, when I lived in New York City and needed to be polished, sophisticated, and well behaved, my dad sent me to Canine College to study good manners. Being a stubborn wirehaired fox terrier, and to my parents' horror, I flunked and had to stay an extra two weeks. Graduation Day came, and I received my diploma for heeling, sitting, and not chewing up Mom's shoes.

For a while I modeled for feature articles in *Country Living* and *Westport* magazines, but I wanted people to know there was more to me than just another pretty face.

Bored to tears watching deer and raccoons in the backyard every day, I decided to find more action in a warmer climate. My goal was to move to Charleston so that I could take advantage of historical sites and smells.

Now, at the ripe age of thirteen, I look forward to spending my golden years here chasing horsedrawn carriages instead of automobiles. My mom, being a Southerner, taught me years ago how to bark "Y'all." But I'm not sure I like beach music nor have I practiced "the Shag," which I've always really thought was a haircut. I do prefer kibble to grits, but, as you can see, I've perfected a grit-eatin' grin!

Must run now. I have a date with a Wheaten to go chase ducks in Waterfront Park.

SOPHIE

BRIX CUMMINGS ("BOO BOO")

It was a rainy Fourth of July when my very special baby, Brix, came to live with me. From the very first we were close. Sometimes it seemed as if he was more than just my new "baby." I would look into his eyes and feel as if there was someone there whom I had always known and loved very much.

Brix was a loving dog; he loved everyone and they loved him. He would sit next to me on the couch with his paw on my shoulder and watch TV. At night he would lie next to me in bed with his paws across my shoulder and his head on mine.

The opening of packages was his favorite thing. (He checked every bag that came into the house.) On holidays and special occasions I always had a living room full of paper pieces. He enjoyed Christmas as much as any child, if not more.

I was blessed to have him with me for eight wonderful years. He developed an incurable illness and died in my arms. I still mourn his loss, but I know that he is smiling and waiting for me at the end of Rainbow Bridge, no longer hurting, but back to the happy, carefree dog he used to be.

There are so many wonderful things that I could say about my "baby," but there is not enough time or space.

CAROL CUMMINGS

ANDY AND KIWI BUNTING

My name is Andy Bunting, and I came into this world on March 7, 2002 (two days before my parents' wedding). My mom told me all she wanted for a wedding gift was a little Yorkie. I actually almost didn't make it to Charleston because my breeder accidentally gave my parents the wrong dog. My parents wanted a little boy, and she gave them a little girl. I still don't know how this mistake wasn't noticed right away. Anyway, about twenty minutes after my parents got on the road with the wrong dog, my breeder realized what had happened. So my breeder and I hopped in the car and raced to Charleston. Three hours later we pulled into my new driveway. I was so excited to switch places with my sister because I had always wanted to be a Charleston dog.

I just loved my new parents and my new home in downtown Charleston. My godmother gave me the best welcoming gift in the world—a brown Burberry bag. I painted the town in that bag on my mommy's shoulder. Every sales lady on King Street knew me, and loved giving me kisses and treats. I also had another bag in which I would go "indognito" on planes, to the beach, and sometimes even into the grocery store. But don't tell anyone about the grocery store because Mom said she could get in trouble.

My life was just perfect until January 19, 2004. Apparently my parents thought that I didn't know how to share with other dogs and that I was a little spoiled. So they got the great idea to get me a sister. And, can you believe, they didn't even consult me on this decision. Everything changed before my eyes. There was this little half-pint puppy named Kiwi getting all the attention. She even tried to jump in my Burberry bag, eat my food, and play with my toys. I didn't like this one bit. I was very mean to Kiwi, which then made my parents very upset at me.

After about a week I realized that Kiwi wasn't going anywhere, so I needed to make the best of this situation. We started to play a little and she wasn't that bad. I could tell she really looked up to me because she copied everything I did. For some reason she also liked it when I licked her face. This was good. I love licking faces, and Mom never lets me lick hers. It was fun going on walks too because we were now the Yorkie posse and could stand up to the other dog posses on our street.

Kiwi has been with us for one year now, and I can honestly say things have changed for the best. Kiwi is definitely my best friend and I love her very much, just as long as she stays away from my food and my Burberry bag. Don't feel bad for Kiwi though—her mom bought her a red coach bag to travel around town. But of course Kiwi still wants to be in my bag with me. When I'm in a good mood, I give in.

ANDY

33

LADY ("LITTLE ANGEL")

Late one stormy afternoon I was on my bike and saw a slender, mostly white, spaniel mix lying on the curb. I assumed that she was dead. When I went to move her to where she wouldn't get crushed, she whined loudly. I wasn't sure what to do—my car had broken down, and the dog cried terribly when I moved away from her. Fortunately I managed to flag down a cab despite a heavy rain.

We went to the old emergency clinic at the west end of the Ashley River Bridge. The vet agreed to treat the lanky spaniel, but she didn't expect me to come back. It was late that night before I could return with my check-book. By the next morning the vet said that the dog would survive and recover.

The lithe mixed-breed was transferred to Dr. Patrick's on Meeting Street. I named her "Lady" and visited her every day. I put up signs and ads in the paper, but no owner turned up. The clinic staff said that Lady was cooperative and even seemed to understand that they were helping her.

Soon Lady was home with me. I have never had a dog who was in my lap or by my side so much. Lady would go into a trance when I rubbed her stomach and would get limp with half-closed eyes. One time at a Folly Beach café, I left her with an employee for a couple of minutes and she cried so loudly that everyone stopped what they were doing. I hurried back and got down on my knees and comforted her, and she quickly regained her composure.

As Lady recovered from her injuries, she started displaying amazing speed and agility. She would run like the wind, then return to me every two or three minutes for some petting, a hug, or a tummy rub. She would jump up and put her paws on my belly, and I never tried to break her of the habit because her touch was as light as a feather. Lady only weighed about twenty-two pounds, but her legs were quite long.

I decided that Lady needed company when I was at work, so I got a Border collie pup from the SPCA. At first Lady was not thrilled with Rob Roy, the Border collie who weighed twenty-six pounds at five weeks and grew rapidly. He pulled her leash, slammed into her, and even drew a little blood with his needle-sharp puppy teeth. Soon she learned to put him in his place. Lady was so quick and agile that she could lunge at him from one side then another often grabbing his hind leg. Even though Robbie soon weighed twice as much as Lady, she could often get him off balance, throw him on his back, and end up triumphantly lying on his chest.

A dark cloud hung over our happy little pack. Lady kept escaping from the yard. She went under the fence, so I reinforced it. She bounced off a bush and over the fence, so I cut down the bush. Finally she learned to jump over a five-foot fence. I needed to stop her immediately, but I was too slow. Lady escaped one too many times, and was killed by a car not far from home.

Several years later Rob Roy sniffed Lady's old sweater. He stared off into space for the longest time. I knew that he remembered Lady. I know that I will never forget her. In the end I had failed my little doggie angel.

DONALD BROCK

VALIANT

My name is Valiant. I am a mixed-breed—part collie and part golden retriever—a mutt to you and, until recently, I felt so myself. I have a happy life now, but before last month it wasn't so good at all.

I can only remember back five or so years. I am eight now I am told, old, but now in quite good health. I used to live in a place called Georgia with many dogs and cats. I lived in a "shelter" run by a very strange woman. She had all of us locked up in tiny cages and fed us just enough to get by. One reason I love other animals so well is that I shared my cage with several dogs, and we decided that if we were going to live, we would have to get along and even love each other. The woman who owned the "shelter" lived far off in California in a very large house, so she never saw us or cared if we lived or died. I am told that she asked kind people for money to help support us, but instead she kept it to buy clothes and go on trips. She was very mean and dishonest to do this, I am told, but I only live one day at a time, as dogs do, and I wouldn't want to be the judge on this.

There were seven hundred animals, and as you can

guess, we made a racket, and were very dirty, dying, and diseased. Some good children saw us and told their mothers, who told a very kind group of people called the SPCA. These people called the police, but before we could be saved, the woman had us all moved to a place called Alabama, where we continued to live in our own mess. "Why would she do this to us?" we asked each other. One wise cat said that she must only do the works of the devil and that she didn't understand that being selfish only leads to misery. We suffered.

One day an amazing thing happened. These men with guns came and arrested the people in charge and closed down the "shelter." Before they could put the woman in jail, she died. She didn't go to heaven our wise cat told us.

So we were all gathered up. I was put in the group that was too old, and I overheard that we were going to be euthanized. But guess what—the men in charge that day got us mixed up with a younger group of dogs and we were put in a truck with a good man driving it. He drove and drove, and when he stopped he would let more animals out. Finally we got to a place called Charleston, and I got out at a shelter called the SPCA. It was good to see the sun and see children who came to adopt the animals. But time passed and no one wanted me. I was hearing sounds in my head that sounded like that word I had heard in Alabama. I was going to be put to sleep, but maybe . . . well, this lady, with a black box around her neck, and her daughter came by and acted like I was real nice—I was clean and my sores were healing. She took pictures. She showed the pictures to a kind man named Robert. This man decided that he would like to give me a home. He talked to his dogs and cats and they said yes!

We have a big yard where we play all day. There is food, and Robert and his friends pat me a lot. I even get to sleep with Robert, and his other dogs love me. So does Robert.

VALIANT

ROSIE

So, Rosie, you've finally put on your wings . . . and I am awed . . . a reaction I never expected, because you've seemed so ready to die. You've been so frail, such a fraction of who you've been . . . deaf, senile (though you've always been a little wacky). So I've gotten used to the fact that you needed to die and that it would happen, and that I might even help it along with a visit to Dr. Patrick . . . to help you return to the state of dignity that you deserve.

My awe . . . what is it about? I think that first it's that you've been such a force, an exuberance, that now a vacuum exists. In all my years of watching and being with you, you just didn't fill a space, you dominated that space and pushed it right into mine—and bit me if it was needed . . . and even did so frivolously, you little devil. You decided what day it was, you determined the ticking of the clock, the rising of the sun. There was no way to halt your force because with you there was no reasoning . . . only teeth. And yet you were fun, an inspiration, in fact. What gusto, and what an ego. You brandished your small self with the swagger of a giant.

I've seen you go after dogs four times your size, and even when you were bested, keep right on. Never say die! You would have taken the fight or stand off into eternity.

I'm beginning to see why I'm awed . . . and it goes even deeper. Once your family learned your ways, they coped the best they could, because there was a dividend. It came in the form of companionship, one of real intelligence. There could never be a moment of loneliness because that white flash of a diversion was always present. There was never a time that a door didn't open, or a dress put on, or a pocketbook picked up that you didn't snatch up the signal . . . we're off! You may as well have been driving the car—you commandeered and oozed superiority.

You were enchanting to your human friends in the way you loved the basics of nature, the things so many take for granted: the motion of leaves, the breeze, the endless interest of fauna. Any animal trespassers that could be within your grasp—you knew their ways, how fast they could run, their bases of safety. And in all the stalking and chasing I never saw you execute one of your prey. I believe it was all sport and not just for yourself. You knew you were being watched by your human friends, admired and enjoyed, providing escapes from the usual goings-on.

I am in awe again for more reasons. Just as this force has been stilled, so has an era, the era—one that represents so much, because your life, Rosie, reached back to that of the eighties—when we had Ben Scott, when things were still functioning in the old classic style at 58 Church. The time of 2:00 dinner, the aromas and chatterings in the kitchen, of trips to Foxbank and patrols in the golf cart . . . of cats in the garden, or no cats

41

because of the white streak . . . of waits for the midday mail and the mailman who turn-tailed and held onto all he valued as he slipped letters through the slot—letters that were ferociously disemboweled and then left to be deciphered . . . of the long watches at various places on the floor where some presumptuous rodent or other had dared to move in, barely separated from a certain end by 250-year-old cypress flooring.

Or of the long wait in the company powder room by the piano tuner. Oh, my Rosie, did you ever show your domination of 58 Church Street then! You had your little tricks you played on Cheeka, and one was with-holding certain bathroom functions and placing them in your special spots—one just under the grand piano. Cheeka forgot to check for your land mines before letting the poor man start his job of keeping the large ebony instrument in perfect pitch for belting out by her of "Mack the Knife" or "60 Minute Man" or "Sleepy Time Down South."

Oh dear, I almost quaver at the thought of finishing the story, needless to say this unsuspecting man started to smell a scent that is unmistakable, and discovered much to his horror that the time bombs had been pressed into the back of his shirt. To his succor came the unshrinking Margaret, long versed in the ways of Rosie, and stripped the poor man of all clothes but his boxers. To hide somewhat his mortification, she led him to the aforementioned powder room, where he waited out the necessarily long cycles of washing and drying of the soiled clothes.

Oh, Rosie, how you loved the cocktail hour at the end of the day, because your Mistress Cheeka was adept at preparing those little snacks that sadly were for others. Was it the little morsel you loved or the trick of the snatch-grab-nab just as company dared so rudely to think of enjoying one. I remember you, Rosie, dangling off the thumb of one unwary guest who had only wanted to accept his hostess' offer of a cheese niblet. In fact all guests were held at bay, left with nothing but conversation, for a change. Such was the classic era of 58 Church Street! Or at least a little sample.

Rosie, this era . . . how could I yearn for it, thinking it was normal? Nothing in your world could bring a usual existence. So I yearn for the world of Cheeka, and your passing-on makes me evermore conscious of its departure.

So my awe . . . is it about peace, is it about loss? I believe it is about memory and recognition of a prize we had in you. You marked a time, a way, and a style. And I don't know how if ever we will find these qualities again all contained in one small white dog—Rosie.

MARTY WHALEY ADAMS

CRICKET NOEL II
("CRICKET")

Hi. My name is Cricket, and I am a miniature schnauzer. I did not have a name the first time I visited Charleston. I was six weeks old, a Christmas present that walked out from under the Christmas tree on Christmas Eve to my papa's surprise in Columbia, South Carolina. When I became my pap's dog, he couldn't think of a name to "fit" me. Christmas day we journeyed to Charleston to a friend's house on Radcliffe Street. There we stayed for a week, and one day during that week we walked to the Battery. I walked as far as I could and "flopped" on the grass at the Catholic Diocese. My papa had to carry me from there on. I was tiny. Seeing me on the ground, he thought of the name "Cricket" (he had played with Buddy Holly's Crickets in his youth). I now had a name.

One year later a moving van came to our house in Columbia and packed us up for our move to Charleston to a very old house, where I could look from the front porch and watch traffic, tourists, and carriages with these big funny-looking dogs they called "horses." One morning, while getting the paper for Papa, I even saw President Clinton come by. (He saw me too.)

I adjusted to Charleston well. I bought a bonnet and would visit regularly the market area, where I would climb up the stairs to each shop, peering in to make sure it was secure and that everyone was happy. Everyone liked my bonnet. I did too. When I did not wear my bonnet, I kept one ear up and one ear down. That was my trademark. Charleston was my city. I loved it and I felt a great responsibility to it.

I thought everyone in Charleston should have a dog to walk, so I wanted to add to the dog population. My mom helped me find Hobbs, my mate. That was not easy. One day at the Harris Teeter we saw a car with seven schnauzers in it. The whole car was barking. We put my papa's business card under the windshield with a note that I wanted a mate. About three months later we got a call from Hobbs's mother. Hobbs came to my house one weekend and I visited his the next. I had three puppies. One moved to South of Broad, one to North Charleston, and my favorite, first born, stayed with me.

I knew many tricks. I could sit, sit up, stand, dance round, roll over, play "dead dog" (lie on my back with my feet in the air), fetch, catch, get Papa's slippers; and I guess my best trick was getting the *Post and Courier* each morning. At least I got the most treats for that. (The Sunday paper was a challenge. It was bigger than I was.)

When I knew I was growing old, I passed on my dog responsibilities to my son, teaching him all my tricks. My parents knew I was not well. I awakened them one Sunday morning to say my good-byes. I am now in the yard of 50 Hasell Street. My portrait (painted by a local artist) hangs in the stairway of 50 Hasell, and from there, even today, I keep a watchful eye.

CRICKET BAILEY

POOGAN

From the moment you step into the parlor of Poogan's Porch there is a pervasive sense of history. The knotted heart-of-pine floors, the dual staircases, and, of course, the first- and second-story porches all reflect the Charleston of days gone by.

Poogan's Porch was originally a spacious, commodious home erected in 1891. By 1976 the character of the neighborhood had changed suitably to allow for the conversion of the house into a restaurant. The last residential owners of the site sold their home and moved away. A little dog stayed behind.

As far as he was concerned, the porch at 72 Queen Street was his. He had been a neighborhood fixture for years, graciously accepting table scraps and back scratches from every family on the block. He was no purebred fluffy puppy; he was a good ol' down-home Southern porch dog. His name was Poogan.

Poogan became the guardian of the fledgling restaurant. From his perch on the front porch he presided over the renovation process, and when we opened our doors for business, he greeted our first guests warmly.

The restaurant family cherished him. He became an institution.

Poogan died a natural death in 1979. We still miss him. This building is his monument.

BRAD BALL AND BOBBIE BALL

DARBY BARTKO ("THE DIVINE MS. DOO")

I hit the lottery! I am so loved, spoiled, and coddled. Who knew life could be so good?

My name is Darby. My mom was a golden retriever, and my daddy, a black Labrador. They were neighbors in Summerville. My brothers, sisters, and I are the result of their second rendezvous.

I am a black beauty of approximately seventy-five pounds—a mixture of the two best breeds, in my opinion. I have short hair, webbed feet, a narrow nose, and affectionate brown eyes. People constantly comment on my good looks. "Oh, what a pretty dog," they say.

My family is a transplant, as ya'll might say. They moved here from Washington, D.C. They have never had a real dog. (Poodles and shelties are toys in my mind.) I don't think they were quite prepared for life with a big dog.

My story is simple. I brought my family closer together. I am the surrogate child-grandchild. Their lives now revolve around me, and I like it that way. I am a constant reminder that life is good. When they watch me chase birds on the beach or see my absolute excitement upon their arrival, they understand that simple pleasures are the most important in life.

Let's talk a little bit more about me, shall we? I am far too special to have just one mommy and daddy. I have several. And I have many friends. Dixie, a four-year-old golden retriever, was my first friend. She has her own pool, which is a major plus. Mason and Dixon, two goldens, are my next-door neighbors. Lady, a rambunctious husky, loves to visit and help me destroy the yard.

I have two houses on the Peninsula, although only one is South of Broad. I also have a beach house at Hilton Head, which my momma purchased shortly after adopting me. (Doggies aren't welcome in rentals.) I absolutely love to swim in pools, lagoons, and especially the ocean. I learned to swim at Hilton Head when I was only six months old. I've always been an overachiever.

I am a professional wave rider now. I even know how to jump the big ones; the trick is to jump straight up and turn your head. I am so well trained that I even wait by the outdoor shower to be rinsed off.

Perhaps my most favorite activity is retrieving, hence my breed's name. I chase anything—birds, squirrels, other dogs, tennis balls, footballs, and any other toy.

I love stuffed animals. My excitement, however, often leads to their demise. I just don't understand that I'm too rough. I have a teddy bear that I bring to bed with me every night. Teddy's new friend is Mobster Lobster, named after a restaurant my parents went to in Key West, Florida. Fortunately my parents continue to indulge my love of stuffed animals, with a continuous supply. (My parents might appreciate donations though.)

Soon I will celebrate my second birthday. I'm anxiously anticipating lots of gifts. But the best gifts of all will be the love and attention I will receive for years to come. Life is good.

DARBY-DOO

SAMANTHA
BERNSTEIN
("SAMI")

My name is Samantha Bernstein, and I am almost seven years old. I am not really a dog. I am really a little girl in a white fur coat. My favorite color is red.

I have a two-year-old sister, Ashley, who follows me everywhere and tries to copy everything I do. I play with her sometimes, but sometimes she is a pain. She likes purple.

My mom makes us get baths and haircuts a lot. Neither one of us likes it, but when we are finished with our beauty treatments we do look pretty. I get red bows in my hair, and Ashley gets purple ones. I think I look prettier than she does.

A year ago I became a registered therapy dog. I visit hospitals and nursing homes. The people always say, "Oh, what a beautiful girl." I like to see the smiles on their faces. I also visit schools and places with special-needs children. They are my favorites. I like to hear them laugh and giggle when I lick them. I have my very own car seat when my mom takes me out in the car. I can look all around because I am so small. I only weigh five pounds. Mom also bought me a little red wagon, and I ride around in it during our visits. I like to ride in my wagon. The children especially like that.

My favorite spot at home when my Dad is at work is on top of the sofa cushions, looking out the window waiting for him to come home. I am always the first one to greet him when he comes home. Ashley tries to get to him first, but I won't let her say hello until after me. After my dad has supper, he and I sit on the sofa and watch TV. I let him watch sports.

A few months ago the doctor told my mom that I have problems with both of my back legs. I have had trouble going up and down the steps when we go out and trouble getting on and off the sofa and the bed. He said I might need an operation on both of my legs. My mom freaked out. She had ramps built so that it is easier for me to get up and down the steps and on and off the sofa and the bed. They have really helped.

Because I have special needs, I like going to see other people who have special needs, and I like making them smile. It makes me happy.

I am a very lucky girl. I love my mom and dad very much (and Ashley too).

SAMANTHA

RUFUS ("TOP GUN")

On a cool spring day I saw him. From across the room, that face, with its bold whiskers and beautiful golden eyes. Hesitant at first, I slowly approached, wary that something that seemed so flawless superficially might be hiding a ferocious behavioral imperfection. He sat pleasantly in his cage and sniffed my hand through the cold impersonal metallic grating. I inquired about his background. He had been given to the shelter because he was simply "unwanted." I wondered how this could be possible as he appeared to have a wonderful demeanor. I asked to take him out of his cage. I was obliged. We walked outside for a bit, and we immediately took a liking to each other. I picked him up in my arms for the first time, and he stared into my eyes as if to say, "Please take me with you."

The deal was sealed. Twenty minutes and one hundred dollars later, we were traveling home . . . together. I refer to him as my "baby boy." I prefer to go nowhere without him. The degree to which I spoil him borders on the outrageous. Frisbee is his own personal passion. He is the most remarkably social and interactive dog I have come across. He has made numerous friends, both canine and human. He has certainly done wonders for my own social life, as I am now well acquainted with all of my neighbors and other local dog owners. We explore all of Charleston together and particularly enjoy Starbucks on Sunday mornings. His name is Rufus, and my life is that much fuller with him at my side.

COURTNEY

CHARLIE
BURBAGE
("TOP DOG")

1997 was a very tearful and a very joyful year. Several tragedies occurred and a brand new life emerged. I had the misfortune of losing my two best friends, Lotus, an Alaskan malamute, and Lakita, my little sharpeii. If that was not enough, I also lost my three cats and my beautiful Shiloh, a strawberry Appaloosa. I still have three other cats, my four rats, and a severe macaw. One afternoon, while cleaning my macaw's cage and replacing the newspapers beneath the cage, I saw an ad in one of the newspapers: "Small black female dachshund mix to good loving home." I thought long and hard about this. I have always wanted a smaller dog and was very partial to dachsies as Mom and Dad raised them when I was child. Alas, I did manage to talk myself out of a new addition—the time was just too soon after the deaths of Lotus and Lakita.

I went on about my life, but three weeks later, again while replacing the newspapers under the bird cage, there was the same ad about that little black dog. Thinking again about this little precious dog, I found myself dialing the phone number of the owner. The day was Sunday when I drove over to meet the little dog. When I arrived the woman took me to her garage and then opened the garage door, from which a little black blur shot out and then ran around the yard like Superman. I had never seen a dog run this fast. When we threw the ball, she just got faster and faster every time she went to retrieve it.

The lady told me about how she had been returning home from the grocery store in the pouring rain when out of the corner of her eye she spotted this small dog crawling out from the woods near her home. Of course she stopped and then coaxed "Charlie" to her. For three months she tried to find the right owner to adopt and give the little dog a permanent, loving home. That Sunday afternoon the lady found who she had been searching and waiting for—me. Charlie and I drove home together, and two lives were changed forever.

In April 1998 I moved to Charleston, and six months later met my husband. Now we three are a big happy family. And as bizarre as it sounds, Charlie and my husband are actually starting to look alike. Charlie is our child and the love of our life.

EVE BURBAGE

ROB ROY MACGREGOR ("ROBBIE," "BIG GUY," "FRISBEE MONSTER")

I first met Rob Roy at the SPCA when I was looking for a companion for my dog Lady. He bounced over to greet me through the bars of his enclosure and nuzzled me for the first time. Twenty-six pounds of black-and-white energy and enthusiasm, he was a five-week-old Border collie, a breed that I was not at all aware of. I had to have him.

I brought Lady to meet the little Border collie. She was not enamored at first. He already outweighed Lady and was clumsy. He slammed into her and bit with his sharp puppy teeth. Using her speed and agility to wrestle him to the ground, Lady soon learned to get the upper hand, sort of. The puppy immediately adored her; she soon liked him.

The fast-growing Border collie actually came with the name "Cedar," but a tree didn't seem like the right name for a furry perpetual motion machine. My father and I watched the movie *Rob Roy*, and it had a Border collie in it. The name of the Scottish hero seemed more appropriate.

I soon learned that Border collies and my Rob Roy were clever and headstrong. The first time that I put him on a leash he decided that he wanted to be the one holding the leash. He once grabbed Lady's leash and "walked" her. Robbie eventually accepted the leash, but still occasionally plays tug-of-war with it when he gets excited.

Border collies also have a strong instinct to herd. Things moving about chaotically get Bob Roy's rapt attention. Then he assumes the classic Border collie crouch reminiscent of a lion that is stalking prey. As a puppy he tried to round up birds on the beach, only to look flabbergasted when they flew away. One time he saw sailboarders darting in and out of a channel and decided to herd them. He started to swim toward them, but was weighed down by his thick wet fur. Robbie didn't give up. He finally found safety in a strip of barely submerged sand that extended far out into the ocean. I had to retrieve him before he got hit by a sailboard.

A great tragedy befell our little "pack" before Rob Roy was three years old. Our dear little Lady escaped from the yard and was killed by a car. When I put her in the grave, Rob Roy lay on top of her and wouldn't let me cover her up. I left him alone, and he eventually covered her with dirt himself. The young Border collie walked as slowly and stiffly as an elderly dog for several days, head bowed and his bushy tail dragging on the ground.

Soon, though, Rob Roy had a new companion—Sirius, a hound-pointer-maybe-spaniel mix. They have been close from the minute they met—wrestling, playing, even grooming each other's fur. They have been a team for seven years now. They have trained together for fly ball, a sort of canine relay. Border collies dominate the sport, but Robbie has been less successful than Sirius because Robbie wants to take off with the ball.

Robbie likes to make his own rules for games and often argues or pouts when he doesn't get his way.

Rob Roy developed a passion for playing with balls instead of, thank God, digging. His greatest dig was while I was preparing to evacuate from Hurricane Floyd. I left the dogs in the backyard for a while, and Robbie must have decided that I might not protect him, so he took matters into his own paws. He dug something that resembled a soldier's underground bunker.

Rob Roy is almost ten years old now and has some arthritis, but the old dog keeps learning new tricks. In recent months he has become a strong swimmer, retrieving balls from the water at Games Island Dog Park. He took up Frisbee three years ago, and this year he has started intercepting other dogs' Frisbees and playing keep-away, thereby earning him the nickname "Frisbee Monster" at the dog park. Recently I have taught him to shake.

I hope that my big, bombastic, fun-loving, and affectionate Border collie keeps his enthusiasm and spirit until the day he dies.

DONALD C. BROCK

SIRIUS THE DOG STAR ("VELVET EARS," "LOUISIANA NUTRIA HOUND")

A group of young boys brought a dog by my house one day. The leader of the group said that his grandmother would only let him keep the dog until they could find a home for it. The youngsters were vague about where they got the dog, but I got the impression that they had rescued the dog from bad circumstances. One chubby lad claimed the dog was a purebred Dalmatian and demanded twenty dollars, but the others told him to shut up.

I said that I already had a dog and that I didn't know if the two together would get along. The leader of the youngsters immediately suggested that I put the two dogs together and see if they liked one another. The two dogs greeted each other and acted like long-lost brothers. I could hardly turn away the new dog. The only trouble I had was that the dog chased Rob Roy, my Border collie, away from his food, snarling like a starving wolf. Despite being larger, Rob Roy just stared at me with pleading eyes, as if to say, "Daddy, do something. This guy is a barbarian." The new dog mellowed when he soon realized that the meals arrived regularly.

I named the new dog "Sirius" after the brightest star in the heavens. Sirius is in the constellation Canis Major, and is also called the Dog Star. My Sirius is about thirty-eight pounds, and has webbed feet and a graceful stride. His fur is short and rather coarse, except for velvety ears. He is white with many black specks and large black patches on his side, head, and the top of his rump.

Sirius has been something of a canine Rorschach blot. Everyone sees their favorite breeds in his ancestry. One dog breeder declared him to be blue tick hound, Walker hound, and beagle. Other people see pointer, spaniel, Dalmatian, and English setter in him. I think that he is just half attention hound and half chow hound.

Sirius and Rob Roy soon became as close as littermates. They lie together, play together, and even groom each other. Their frenetic play often looks and sounds like a real fight, but the violence is fake. I call it professional dog wrestling.

Recently my father's miniature schnauzers, Max and Fritz, started meeting my dogs at Games Island Dog Park. The little "ankle biters" adore cousin Sirius and come running to meet him.

Sirius has hunting-dog instincts and a scent-hound nose, but few opportunities to pursue prey. One time a cat got in his yard and wouldn't leave. Sirius crouched down in front of it and barked furiously, careful to stay out of reach of its claws. Rob Roy crept up behind the cat and nipped the tip of its tail, sending it over the fence. The dogs couldn't have been more proud if they had routed a tiger.

Sirius has learned fly ball, a canine hurdle race where the dogs retrieve a ball from a spring-loaded box. At first Sirius had no interest in balls, but there was a reliable way to motivate him—food.

For all his activities, Sirius' favorite thing is being petted. Each morning he presses his chin on my knee when

I put on my shoes and socks. Each evening he puts his head on my arm while I watch TV. He takes my slightest gesture to be an invitation to get in my lap. Nor is he shy about finding new human friends. Sirius is a true attention hound.

DONALD C. BROCK

SADIE
GREENBERG

My name is Sadie and I am not a Charleston dog. I am "from off," as Charlestonians like to say. The people I own bring me here every weekend. I am fifteen years old, but everyone thinks I look much younger. I love walking on the Battery and chasing other dogs off of Longitude Lane. I used to go shopping with my mother until I pee-peed on the rug in Berlin's and excited the poodles at RTW. My very favorite thing to do is to take Saturday afternoon naps with my dad. My family loves me so much that they had my portrait painted by Marty Whaley Adams.

SADIE

BELLA GABRIELLA OF CHARLESTON ("GABBY")

Hi, my name is Gabriella, which, I believe, means "spoilt rotten" in English. I love big people, belly-rubs, and my new mom 'n dad. I don't understand "little people" or other dogs. They're all beneath me (sniff). There are some that fascinate me sometimes, but I don't know why. It must be something to do with the way they sniff me.

Mom picked me from my sisters because I was the smallest and cutest, and she was undergoing something called "chemotherapy." Dad was away, traveling in Europe for an extended period. He's a sailor, you know. Mom said that she wanted my company more than his. Which is as it should be. I thought she would upset Dad when she said that we're both "runts," but she loves us both the same. And I don't know what a runt is, anyway. I guess it looks like Dad.

I parade down Queen Street to Waterfront Park nearly every day, where I see how many times I can have a belly-rub. There's nothing quite like having my feet in the air with a stranger rubbing my little pink belly. I call it "mutual gratification." My mom and dad have met some wonderful people here, while I've met some amazing seagulls and pigeons, and we play "I chase, you fly." Oh boy! . . . and the smells . . . I can be burrowed into the bushes and lampposts for hours at a time (if they'd let me).

My favorite people include Officer Simmons, who I first met in Waterfront Park when I was six weeks old and no bigger than my mom's hand. She still says "hi," and when she isn't looking, I leave a part of me running down some shady tree. I do, however, have a "crush" on Harry, a little Norwich terrier who lives by the park, and I always look out for him.

I am the most beautiful bichon frise in the world, and although I'm on the small side, I have a heart as big as the world. I love everyone. So does Dad, but Mom said that he'd get a similar "cut" to me, if he tried to.

Now, I know that I'm not a "macho" dog, and in fact I love cuddling and being cute, but a funny thing happened the other day while in the park with Dad. After a string of leggy, muscular males walked by—and I was quite weak and breathless—a really cute fifteen-year-old girl walked up to Dad, and to his horror, in her breathless Southern whisper, said, "Mah Daddy says that it takes a Real Man to walk a dawg like that." He went red and guffawed with laughter, and if I didn't know better, he tried to hide me in his shirt. Then I got a quick ride home, which was fine, because there weren't too many "stomach-rubbers" around.

It was three days before he took me out again. I don't know why. Although they are simple folk, I love them. . . . And should there be any belly-rubbers out there, I love you too.

GABBY

64

ATHENS
("A")

For nearly a year I was passed from one family to another. Everyone thought I was really cute, but no one seemed able to understand that puppies have lots of energy, and sometimes we're naughty and like to chew anything we can find. Hey, we get bored when there's no one around to play with us.

So once again I broke through the screen on the porch while my newest family was away at work. I didn't realize then how close I was to the highway and how dangerous things like that could be. I just wanted to get free and explore. Since I was fascinated by a big building next to our house, I decided to sniff it out. After an hour or two, I was worn out, so I stopped to rest on a nice soft mat in the sun.

I was almost asleep when a door suddenly opened and there stood a fat man with white hair and a white beard who looked just like Santa. He seemed really nice as he bent over to pet me and check my collar. Unfortunately my tag was gone, so he didn't even know my name. He gently invited me into his house as he quickly closed the door behind me. He even gave me some food and water. It tasted good since it had been a busy morning. He then started to make signs telling people that he found me. He told me that he would try to get me home safely. I really liked him.

After two days he did find the people who knew me, but by then I think that he wanted to keep me. At least I hoped he did. When my old friends told him that they weren't sure if they could really care for me anymore, my new friend immediately said that he had already fallen in love with me and would like to keep me. That made me really happy. My new friend even gave me a neat new name. He calls me "Athens."

I loved my new home and my new name and especially the fact that my new friend worked from home, so he was around a lot. But, I have to admit, when he was gone I still liked to chew things—lots of things, like his old shoes and even his new mattress. At one point I was afraid that I was in a lot of trouble and my new friend might not want to keep me anymore. But, instead, he went out and bought me a present—a really large cage in which he puts blankets and lots of my toys. Oh yeah, he puts me in there too whenever he leaves the house. I like it. It's like having my own special space inside our home; and now, when he comes back, he knows I've been a good dog.

I really love living here. And every night when I curl up next to my new dad, I know I am finally home.

ATHENS

RED
("BANDIT,"
"REDLY")

Red is a sweetheart indoors, but turns into a madman once he is outside. He is a top-notch escape artist, who can climb trees, jump over fences, open car windows, and sneaks his way out into the wide-open world any time he has a chance. He patiently waits and watches until he sees the door open for a second too long or the moment when I loosen my grip on his leash, and then bam, he's off.

One day last September, Red was getting a bath outside after a trip to the beach. As I was about to dry him off, I turned around to grab the towel and loosened my grip on his collar. A second later Red was gone. I ran from the yard to the street and saw Red streaking—soaking wet—across Bull Street. I chased him down the street and saw him turn into a backyard. Phew, I thought, I'll just try to corner him and hope the people who live there don't notice me running around their backyard chasing my crazy dog. As I turned into the yard I noticed a huge party going on and a bunch of women standing around in matching dresses. How strange, I thought, until I turned around and saw the bride hiding behind her bridesmaids. Everyone turned to me and started yelling, "This is a wedding. We're

67

about to start. Get your dog." I stood frozen for a minute and then all I could think was, How could he have picked this backyard? All the backyards in Charleston to choose from, and he decided to choose the one with the wedding, just before the bride walks down the aisle. I immediately started searching for Red, but noticed the caterers were already trying to corner him in the bushes. The ushers immediately raced over to help wrangle the crazy dog—my dog, who decided it would be fun to crash the wedding. Suddenly the music stopped and the guests all turned around just in time to catch a glimpse of Red as he ran down the aisle, stopped to catch his breath, smiled at his audience, and ran back down the aisle toward the cake.

A horde of men in tuxedos lured him away from the cake and chased him around another lap of the backyard while the wedding photographer chased after all of them snapping pictures. I ran back toward the bushes, and an usher and I cornered Red between a rose bush and a fence. Red took one look at the situation, saw his only chance for freedom, and bolted straight out of the comer between the two of us. Luckily another usher was positioned right behind us and tackled Red. Everyone around us breathed a huge sigh of relief and started clapping. Mortified, I apologized for postponing their wedding and quickly escorted Red out of the backyard. I passed the bride on the way out, and profusely apologized again, but all she could do was laugh. She came over to pet Red, thanked him for entertaining her guests, and then, however, added that he was not invited to the reception.

MARISA CONNORS

BENJAMIN

My name is Benjamin of Charleston, and I am a black cocker spaniel. When I was nine months old, I was given to the SPCA for readoption, and I don't know why. But on my first birthday a new lady came to take me. I loved my new home with Jean-Lawrence De La Poer, but I felt lost and knew something was still wrong. Luckily I had my AKC papers with the names of my sire, Gallant Mr. Beasley, and my mother, Lady Buffy O'Malley, and the name of my breeder, Mr. Joseph Baumil. So, we went for a visit to see them. Gallant Mr. Beasley was brought in first to a glass, partly opened, patio door. First, he sniffed at me through the small opening, and then he put his paw to the glass. So I sniffed back and put my paw to the glass—he knew me and I knew him. Next, Lady Buffy O'Malley was brought out. We also sniffed through the opening. Then she tossed her head a bit as if to say I am your mother, you are fine, Benjamin, now go on about your business. And, so I did, happy and made whole again.

My new life included five acres of plantation yard to run on. I was given tennis balls for my first present and a strange-looking machine that would throw the balls to me and fill up again. We also had a wonderful house in town, and I often kept company with our housekeeper, Mary Ellen Jackson. My favorite activity was to line up all my balls and bark at her until she would throw them for me while she vacuumed. She never rested while she worked, and I didn't either. So, I would rapidly retrieve the balls, one and all, and line them back up for her. I never got tired of doing this, and I guess Mary Ellen didn't either!

I also loved being the family protector. Whenever I heard the trashmen coming, I put myself on full alert. I was able to stand my ground in the courtyard, where I could see them through the iron grill in the gate, which was just at my eye level. After delivering a full chorus of insults, I could race up the stairs to the second level, dash through the house, and then make it to the balcony on the front just in time to finish them off before they rounded the corner for the next house. This was an exhilarating experience for me, and was frequently augmented when I was in the car and saw them in another neighborhood, where I once again exchanged salvos. There were many smiles from all.

After dark, however, I switched roles—I became protector of the hearth rather than the family. This was a late evening activity in which I took great pride. I would station myself on the first landing platform on the staircase. After dark no one was going to enter this house without my express consent. Whoever came in had to make it past me. So, as soon as I heard the key in the door I began my onslaught. My new family would have to make a dash for the elevator door on the first floor before I could make it down the steps. If they were lucky enough to get in it before I could catch them, I would then race back up the stairs as the slow-moving carriage made its way up to the second or third floors. They would flee to their rooms and barricade themselves in until the sun came up the next morning, and I once again went back to my role of protector of the family.

I had a wonderful life.

BENJAMIN

LUCKY

"You should name him 'Lucky.' He certainly is lucky to have found you." This was our daughter Kim's observation after she saw the addition to our family. Through the years this observation has been reversed. We are the lucky ones to have found him.

We first came in contact with Lucky in October of '94. Six months before, we had moved from New Jersey to South Carolina. Our darting Welsh terrier, Simon, had died a month before we moved. My husband, Joe, did not want to entertain the idea of getting another dog. He noted that we had plans to travel now that we were retired.

After six months I finally wore Joe down. How could we possibly live without a dog? We decided to visit new vets who had opened a business with a separate but attached boarding and grooming building, a pet store, and a vet's office.

Our first stop was to the office of Dr. Steele and Dr. Senf. We had a number of questions to ask them. What are some good breeds for the Southern climate? Are Jack Russells really feisty? We had just gone through thirteen years of "feist" with our Welsh terrier. We were looking for a little more sedateness in our next choice.

The vets told us to go next door and talk to the owner of the pet shop. She was raising several breeds herself. She was delightful and most informative. She loved Doxies and Boykins. Then she proceeded to make the statement that changed our lives. "It's too bad you aren't interested in a year-and-a-half-old male cocker spaniel who has been severely neglected. We both looked at each other and said we would love to see him."

She took us back to the vet's office and then into the hospital section. One of the vets gave us the history behind this sad little dog's story. Someone had taken him to their office and asked what the problem was with this little dog. The sight of him sickened the vets and their technicians. He had no hair, scratched incessantly, and his horrible odor was beyond belief. The vet told the person who had brought him in that the dog was very ill and just from a brief observation had many problems. The vets knew that they would not see that person again.

Lucky was a very sick dog, almost to the point of death. He had the mange so badly that the technicians had to wear masks when they were anywhere in Lucky's vicinity because of the odor.

They had discussions over his prognosis, and they came to the sad conclusion that maybe the best option would be to put him out of his misery, especially after finding out that he had heartworm. This illness had all been caused by the neglect of people chaining him outside, never letting him in the house. He suffered through summers, winters, and dark and frightening nights.

Rose, the manager of the boarding complex, was observing all this. Everyone's heart was broken because he was so sweet. Rose noticed the little tail that kept wagging whenever someone said a kind word to him. How could any animal with such a gentle spirit, after extreme neglect, not be given some chance?

"Why don't I take him way in the back of the boarding facility and see if the special baths might help the mange? What do we have to lose?"

Everyone quickly agreed that that was worthwhile. Lo and behold, after a short time his skin looked so much better and the odor disappeared. The vets were amazed. They decided to try to medicate his heartworm. It was either a kill or cure proposition. Rose kept him in the back room, taking him over to the vets for the needed medication. He was on the road to recovery when we first saw him. The vet took him out of his crate. It was love at first sight. We knew we had found the right one to share our lives.

I didn't think he was a cocker spaniel. His paws were much too large and his body seemed too long. The doctors assured us that he was definitely a cocker. The fact that he had no hair made him look that way. He probably won't have any hair because his mange was so devastating, they told us.

We told them that we wanted him, but we would take him home when he was well. We would pay for his medical bills. We left and went home. In an hour we were back at the kennel. We would like to take him home now, we announced. Rose was thrilled. She got him all ready with lots of directions from the vets for his medications.

We changed his name. Rose had called him "Joe Cocker." Since we had one Joe already, a new name was a necessity. I began to pick the tiny scabs he had all over his back and ears. Every time I picked one off, hair would appear the next day. After a week of this, Lucky had a beautiful coat of hair.

Lucky has been a shining light in our lives. He has done amazing things in the twelve years that we have been together. He is an excellent agility dog, winning awards. He shares his generous spirit with all who meet him. Lucky is also a registered therapy dog. We visit MUSC Children's Hospital, and he brings a smile to the very ill. Lucky visits schools, sometimes with ten children at one time, touching his ears, hugging him, as he patiently lets them enjoy him. Sometimes these are children who are very fearful of dogs.

At the VA Hospital Lucky lies with patients on their beds. He also visits a local nursing home, weekly. Last but not least, he is a part of the Woof Program at the Mitchell School. Lucky listens as students read a story to him. Sometimes his head is on their laps.

Lucky is probably fourteen years old. He likes to sleep a lot now, but he still has a busy social life as one can see. He is so special to us. Every day we thank Rose and the doctors for not going with their first conclusion. Now you know why we are the lucky ones.

PAT AND JOE DISCHINO

LADY HANCOCK
("LADY-LOVE")

I came to Charleston under very unique circumstances. I was living in Fayetteville, North Carolina, with a young man who was deployed to Iraq. Before departing, he dropped me off at the local community hospital. He told me that the animal shelters were overloaded and that he thought I might be able to find a loving family there.

Being a self-assured Siberian husky, I strutted straight into the hospital lobby and caught the elevator. When I got off on another floor, a senior citizen volunteer noticed me. He instantly fell in love with my startling blue eyes. Mr. Hancock spent the following two weeks trying to locate my owner.

Fortunately he was unsuccessful and decided I would be the perfect Christmas present for his daughter. After the holidays, my new mom drove me to my new home in Charleston, where my life as "Lady" began.

Upon arrival at a cat-dominated household, I quickly disrupted the quiet and organized way of life that my mom—and her four cats, two of which are deaf—had grown accustomed to. I have certainly made Mom's life more adventurous. I like nonstop activity.

With the help of a local pet communicator, the youngest deaf cat named Christopher became my puppy trainer. He never let me out of his sight. He still doesn't hesitate to smack me around either, which is quite ironic considering that I now weigh sixty-four pounds. We are good friends, often seen wrestling and playing tag in the backyard.

The house leader is named King. He's from the Himalayas and wears a mask. I've tried to be a friend, but he says that dogs are not worth his time and he has no time for me.

I have settled in well to life in Charleston. I go to doggy daycare in Mt. Pleasant four times a week. A teenage girl who lives in my neighborhood takes me for walks along upper King Street. All the merchants know me. Another one of my neighbors is a triathlete. He takes me for long runs around the Battery. He has even invited me, but not my mom, to accompany him on a ski trip this winter. I can't wait to frolic in the snow.

Because I have so many toys and need some travel comfort, my mommy bought a new SUV just for me. She drives me everywhere in it. One of my favorite stops is the East Bay dog park. I have my own doggy social club there. It's funny—I have a much more active social life then my mommy does.

And I have more friends, especially if you count my fuzzy stuffed animals. I have at least twenty, and my toy selection is often a good indicator of my mood. When I'm pouting I always choose to play with my yellow duck. And when the cats get too close to my precious toys, I suspiciously take an inventory.

At the end of the day I head to my canvas crate, where

I can be found sleeping with legs up in the air, usually accompanied by Jazz, who wisely chooses to sleep on top of my crate.

LADY HANCOCK

CHARLESTON DOGS

Charleston is a lot like Heaven,
with sparkling waters crashing
against sandy beaches
where dogs love running best.

Not too far away there are fields. Fields and
    fields and fields.

When a dog first comes to the beach,
    he just runs.

Charleston has Colonial Lake and ponds on
Daniel Island
    filled with geese who honk and
dance and tease. The dogs love this.

They run beside the water and bark
and bark and sometimes they jump in.

There are children.
    Of course.
Charleston children.

Dogs love children
more than anything else in the world (except
    fresh fragrant hot soft bread)
so it's a good thing that Charleston is filled
with plenty of them.

There are children on bikes and
children on boats. There are children throwing
    big yellow fuzzy tennis balls
and children kayaking on Shem Creek.
The dogs are there, and the children love them
dearly.

And oh,
    the dog biscuits.
Biscuits and biscuits
    as far as the eye can see.

Dog bakers have a sense of humor, so
they make the biscuits in funny
shapes for the dogs.
There are kitty cat biscuits and
squirrel biscuits, ice cream sundae
biscuits and Southern ham biscuit biscuits.

Every one who passes by
has biscuit for a dog.

And, of course, all Charleston's dogs
sit when the children say "sit."

Every dog becomes a good
    dog in Charleston.

Clouds turn inside out to make fluffy beds for the
    dogs in Charleston,
and when they are tired from running and
barking and eating Southern ham biscuit biscuits,
    the dogs each find a cloud bed for sleeping.

They turn around and around
in the cloud
    until it feels just right,
and then they curl up
and they sleep.

God watches over each one
    of them.
And there are no bad dreams.

Dogs in Charleston
almost always
belong to somebody.

And, of course,
the dogs know this. But
    Charleston is full of beckoning adventures.

So sometimes a dog will take a little walk
    by himself
through the neighborhood for a little visit and
quietly, almost
invisibly, the dog will sniff about his neighbor's
backyard,
will investigate the cat next door, will follow a child
to school,
will sit on a front porch and wait for the mail.

When he is satisfied that all is well,
    the dog will return home.

It is where dogs belong,
at home, with those who love him.

All dogs in Charleston
have people who love them and
who give them special names.

Their homes have yards and porches
and there are couches to lie on
and tables to sit under while
children eat their dinners.

There are special bowls
with the dogs' names on them.

And each dog is petted and reminded
how good he is, all day long.

Dogs in Charleston may stay as
long as they like and this
can mean forever.

They will be there when old friends
show up. They will be there
at the door.

Charleston dogs.

VICKI FAITH

BUCKSHOT'S LITTLE GRIFFIN ("GRIFFIN")

I am a beautiful blonde. I have long, fluttery eyelashes that float like butterflies over the pools of melting chocolate that are my eyes. My amazing smile glitters as I seduce my next target. My waist is fashionably nipped in and my nails are always perfect.

I love to investigate people, places, and things. Of course flawless good looks can only help a girl achieve her secret missions. It never seems to hurt that I also have a knack for charming unsuspecting souls into submission. Or that I claim Charleston as my home.

This story I am about to tell you has to be true because even a fabulous storyteller like me couldn't spin this windy. It all begins here in the Lowcountry, a moist, breathing, slumbering place, where spits of no-see-um infested, live oak–draped land reach like the toes of a Labrador's paw into fragrant, pulsing, golden apple marshlands. Even the air can be sliced with the twist of a good Frisbee throw.

The family was gathered on the front porch of the big house (that would be the water side of the house for y'all from off) celebrating my birthday. The velvety lawn rolled gently down to the battered seawall—of course built with old Charleston bricks—and access to an old wood dock stretched beyond. It seems like an innocent enough place for the tale to begin, but here

83

we are and it's all I can think about—that is, what transpired to bring us to this moment to begin with. I am consumed and, you'll see, I'm totally entitled.

Think about it. There are those moments in your life that you never see coming, a pivotal moment that will change your life forever. Yet, you never see it. Until it's too late. Well, when I first arrived here three and a half years ago, I never dreamed that I would be immersed here enjoying all this.

Oh, cats, here comes Lucky. Excuse me for just a moment.

"Hey, Grif, whatcha doing? Can I help? I know I can. Please let me help." He gave me a sloppy wet kiss and a huge hug.

I could never stay mad at Lucky. He's my brother, a bit goofy sometimes, but always well meaning. Besides, he smelled really good. I was dying to find out where he'd been and what he'd been up to without me. Before I could ask, he bounded away to check on the pack of foxes that lived at the pool house.

Where was I? Oh, yeah! The pivotal moment! My pivotal moment, you see, Lucky—he's my little brother—is the brother that almost wasn't. At a young age I had lost brother and sister. See, because of circumstances beyond my control, most of my siblings were put up for adoption and moved to new homes when they were just forty-nine days old. Lucky and me included. I was adopted right away, but not Lucky. He spent the first night with our dad and Sunny, one of our sisters. He woke me up early the next morning with a frantic phone call begging me to come and get him. There was blood everywhere, he cited, and Sunny was gone! He was terrified that he'd be next!

I knew that was some bodacious bullhockey because

my brother was generally regarded as the "precious little baby" and no harm could possibly come to him. Only the best for little brother. I guess you'd think that sounds like a classic sibling rivalry thing, but, if you knew certain things, you'd agree with me. Besides, that would change soon enough.

Did I tell you that I am a beautiful blonde?

GRIFFIN

LUCKY

At forty-nine days, all of the puppies in my litter piled into the back of a big black Suburban for a ride. We were a mass of squiggling, squirming, licking, jumping puppy fur, all eyes, ears, wet noses, and wagging tails.

What a grand adventure we had set out on. After a short ride and a stop for hot dogs, we all tumbled out of the big truck into the most beautiful place on earth—Charleston. Green grass as far as the eye can see, grand slopes for rolling, big trees, little squirrels, and our very own swimming pool (well, that's what we thought). We ran and played and rolled and ran some more. And napped. We napped a lot.

Slowly throughout the afternoon, parents came to take their new babies home. Soon it was just two of us left. I kept hoping that someone would pick me, but they didn't. I wasn't too sad because I still had my sister to play with, and I believed with my whole heart that I would find someone special to love me. Eventually we both tuckered out and collapsed on the floor inside her new house to sleep.

I woke up early the next morning, excited about the prospects of the day. But somehow, someway, the day went hideously wrong. Something awful happened to my sister, and I was whisked away quickly to stay with another yellow sister, Griffin, and Vicki. It was just a temporary situation, until someone special came to adopt me and I would have a home of my own.

Months passed. Several people came to see me, but some didn't like me, and I didn't like others. Twice I was beaten up by a bigger dog during overnight stays and had to be rushed to the emergency room. Once I even had a tooth knocked out. I came back to Griffin and Vicki's bloodied and battle-worn.

Meanwhile I was adjusting to living with Griffin and Vicki. We played hard and learned some manners and became close. Even though my days were filled with happiness, my nights were black. I worried what would become of me if no one wanted me—ever.

One day, after a long walk and a romp, Vicki sat down with Griffin and me to tell us what my future would be.

"Sweet pea" (that's what she calls me sometimes), she said, "you've been a very good boy and we love you lots. The time has come to make a decision about your future."

I was kind of scared. I loved it here and I worried that my next home wouldn't be the same. I hated those overnight stays.

Did this mean that I would go to the pound or be sold to the highest bidder? I was really nervous.

"I've searched my heart," she continued, "and de-cided that you belong with Griffin and me. So we are going to keep you forever and forever."

I was so *happy*! I jumped all over the place and barked with glee. I couldn't lick them enough. All this time and I was *home* all along!

Life is good. They tell me every day how special I am and how much they love me. And that we will always be together. I believe.

LUCKY

Buckshot Faith ("Buck")

Love to run. Love to play hard. Love, love, love to steal bread off of the countertop. Wag my tail lots and lots. And my entire back end, including my tail, goes in happy circles. Kiss people I love on the face. Sometimes get in trouble for being overly enthusiastic with the love.

Love to hunt. Wow, really truly love to hunt. Hunt Canadian geese. Hunt snow geese. Hunt mallard ducks. Well, truthfully, hunt any kind of ducks. Hunt quail. Hunt pheasant. Hunt rabbits. Love the big bang and go. Go fast. Run hard. Catch the bird. Sometimes swim. Maybe get two birds at once. Fun in feathers. Bring the birds back and go for more. Birds. Birds. Birds. Hunt!

Love to chase other things too. Love to chase rabbits. And crabs. Ouch! Sometimes chase flopping fish. Love to chase foxes and cats. Yes, cats. Never catch them. Love to chase kids. Fast, screaming, bouncing little kids. Pass them by. Love to run, ears spread like wings. And balls. Love to chase balls. Big balls, little balls, soccer balls. Any balls.

And cuddle. Love to cuddle. Full-body hugs, go-for-the-face kisses. Especially in bed—someone else's bed.

Not mine. The good bed with all the fluffy pillows and feather comforters and the oh-so-soft sheets. Stretching out. Taking the whole bed for myself. Yeah. That feels good. Tickle my toes. Snuggle up with me, the big brown dog.

Love to eat. Will eat most anything. Dog food. Dog biscuits. Especially bread. Yum! Slurp oysters with the crowd. Steaks, lamb, hamburgers, macaroni and cheese that the kids set down too close to my nose. Or not. Maybe they just looked away. Sneak eats. Cat food. Wow, that's hard to beat. And it's so plentiful around my house. Potato chips. Not really too picky. People don't always approve of my sneak eats. Well, okay, *never* approve of my sneak eats. Sometimes it gives me tummy problems. Yuck. But it's always worth it.

Love to ride. In airplanes. Especially the ones where I meet the pilots. In cars that go fast. In trucks that jump through the brush to the best hunting places. In people's arms who love me. In flat boats that go on the water to a secret blind. In family boats that tour the harbor. In big boats that glide across the water smooth as a duck.

Swimming is good. In the stinky, pluff-muddy marsh. Or the salty harbor. At the beach, crashing through the waves, water stinging my eyes. Swimming. Soaking the coat, using the tail as a rudder. Going after the birds or just goofing around. Getting muddy or taking a bath. Swimming in a pond or a pool. It's all good. Never too much water.

Love to sleep and nap. Nap in the car or at home. After a hard day of work or play. Love to nap at the office or at home. Love to curl up in the middle of the hall at home in the middle of everything and sleep. Snoring loudly. Sometimes drooling. Love to sleep on my bed or on the couch. Even on the floor. Especially if there is a rug or a carpet or something soft.

Love to run. Run through the cornfields of dreams. Young, healthy, happy. Eyes sparkling. Embracing life. Running. Hunting. Chasing. Cuddling. Eating. Lots of eating. Riding. Swimming. Sleeping. The life of a Charleston dog.

BUCK

I'M JUST WILD ABOUT HARRY ("HARRY")

My name is Harry. This comes from my grandmother, who thought that I was way too cute to be called Truman. Formally I'm registered as "I'm Just Wild About Harry," but who goes on formality? As I lie here in the kitchen between two air conditioning ducts, I can't help but think, What am I doing here in Charleston?

I am an 180-pound St. Bernard. My ancestors rescued people in the cold mountains of Switzerland. They braved the harsh freezing weather to save climbers who got caught in avalanches. St. Bernards were strong and gentle. They carried kegs of brandy around their necks to help restore warmth to freezing bodies. I am strong and gentle. I have a keg. Mom puts ice water in it in the summer when we walk in the heat. I think something is lost here.

I came here from Michigan, big dog country! I have vague memories of wonderful cold weather. I would leap into huge drifts of snow and slide down the icy driveway. I never could understand why Mom wanted to go back in the house after only an hour of fun in the snow. I got the feeling she and I had different ideas of fun.

I live with Mom, Dad, and two cats. For the most

part we all do pretty well. The cats love me, as well they should. I am an amazing pet. I tolerate them because, after all, we are family. When it comes to dinner, however, it's every man, err, dog, for himself.

We travel a lot and I love the car. I get extra treats and lots of attention at motels. One day I hopped in the back seat and we drove for two days. When we arrived in Charleston, I jumped out of the car and into the heat. The vacation was great. It did seem unusually long. Each time I got in the car for a ride, I ended up still in Charleston. Hey, wait a minute, where is the snow? After a year of this "vacation," I figured I was not going home. I am quite handsome, not necessarily brilliant.

So here I am, a cold-weather dog in Charleston. When I first moved here, a man described me as a "heap of dawg!" Right away I knew this was not the same as the cold North. So what's a dog to do? We walk a lot and I get lots of attention. Children hug me, adults pet me, and some offer me treats. Because I am so big, there are many who have to be coaxed over, only to learn that I am as sweet as I am huge. My idea of a great day is playing with all my friends at the dog park. We chase balls and run in circles. It's a very full afternoon. In a dog's eyes, the parks where we can run and run are the best part of Charleston. Mom says the history and restaurants are the best part. But what does she know, she doesn't even like snow!

HARRY

St. James Electric Slide ("Emily")

I am a German shepherd, and I grew up as an only puppy. Everyone calls me Emily, and there is some dance called the Electric Slide that is part of my registered name. Go figure!

My mom is very proud of me because I was her first German shepherd to ever win a championship point at a dog show. She tells me she tried and tried for years, but I finally did it for her. She has gone on now to showing some little dogs called Tibetan spaniels. I guess that is a good thing. I liked to travel, but I am one of those who like to potty at home, so traveling really is not all that much fun for me.

I am eight and a half years old now and am still full of mischief. When I was very young, I pulled a sock off my human little brother's foot. He was not happy, but the grown-ups thought it was too funny. What did he expect—he was sitting on the couch with an extra bit of sock sticking off the end of his foot. I had to do it! Oh, yes, don't ever leave any men's underwear lying around. I like to grab it and run. I am also real good at finding missing items under beds.

Speaking of those little dogs, I have become quite

the disciplinarian with them lately. The oldest female likes to pick fights with the oldest male over food of all things. The last time she did it, I just put my paw on her and she had to stop. Once, I also stopped the other female from sneaking into the house by putting my paw on her, too.

Even though I am getting older, I still love toys that squeak. I will grab one up on my way outside, but my mom always stops me from getting it outside. Not too long ago, I was able to sneak one by her. It was not even a squeaky toy, but some silly Winnie the Pooh puppet that one of those little dogs loves. We all had a good time with that thing in the backyard for about a week. Then I delivered the head to my mom one day while she was sitting on the deck. She was not a happy camper.

Recently my mom consulted a "pet communicator" about one of the little males. During the course of her consultation, she figured out that I have been communicating things to the little guy. I told him to be careful on tables and that he might fall off. Needless to say, that did not make my mom very happy with me. She wants this guy to love being on the table. I will never understand all that.

I guess I should also tell you that I am really bad about climbing the fence to get into the pen with my son. Sometimes his brother visits, and I like to spend time with both of them. Well, really I am checking to see if they have any food left in their bowls. I am still full of mischief and will never pass up the opportunity to pick up a toy or even raid the trash can in the kitchen. I will probably never grow up. There is no fun in that!

EMILY

EDISTO
HERRING

I sure hope they can see me. I'm so small. I can see them from here. They look okay. No kids with them. That's a good sign. Nice car, soft voices. Let me see if I can get a little closer to where they are standing. What are they doing up here anyways. Probably camping or something. I'm hungry. Okay, so, I hope I look okay. These fleas are eating me alive, not to mention this rash I have going on. What am I thinking? They probably already have a pet. Oh, oh, oh . . . she sees me. Here she comes! What should I do? Hide? Run!

Chicken . . . her hand smells like chicken. Yummy! I'm scared. I can't get close. Sniff sniff sniff. What's this . . . she's motioning for me to come closer. Oh, that feels so good on my back . . . my ears, under my jaw. Yeah, I could get used to this. Quick, run away. No, go back to her. Food. Fresh water. I think I'll hang out here. She hasn't taken her eyes off of me. She's very curious about me.

What's that noise? It sounds familiar. Wait a minute. What's gotten into me? I'm letting her pick me up. I'm sitting on her lap. A boat? She is taking me on a boat ride down the Edisto River. I'm scared, but her arms and hands make me feel safe, plus, my tummy is full. The fresh air feels great! So many things to see and smell! What a smooth ride. Look over there on the bank of the river . . . you can see where I live. Hey, look at me! I'm riding in a boat!

Whew! Back on dry land. She won't let me down from her lap . . . and I'm not going to argue with her. It feels nice and warm and safe. I'm tired. I think I'll rest now. She's getting up again and taking me with her. The car? I have the entire back seat to myself. Feels pretty good. What's going on here? Where am I going now?

Soft carpet, fresh towels, water, and food two inches from my nose, something to chew on, and some ticking-noise thing that reminds me of my mommy. Do I live here now? I'm scared, but happy to be out of the heat and inside. She's constantly checking on me, holding me and talking to me. I sure do have a lot to learn about this new way of life. I think I hit the lottery. She even gave me a piece of jewelry . . . a necklace with a charm on it. Cool! I wear it every day.

Well, that's my story of how me and my family came to be on the banks of the Edisto River when I was about five months old. I'm so glad they found me! They are great people who initially put up with a lot from me— all the chewing, whining, digging, and destroying I did until I finally settled down and realized that this family was the "real deal." Today some things have changed from the first day that I arrived. For example, I ride in a bigger boat now, I have a bigger yard to play in, I have three siblings (one canine, one cat, and one human), and I even have my own chair to lounge in when a good movie is on. What remains the same is the love and attention I get from my family. My name is Edisto and I love my family.

EDISTO

THE LITTLE WHITE DOG ("FRIEDA")

If you look at my picture, I'm not a little white dog, and that's the whole point of my story. I was a rescue, but not an official rescue with groups and fosters and a true organization. I was rescued by a clinic staff and then a couple, who once had a little white dog.

They aren't sure about all the details of my early life, and I've put most of them out of my mind. The first people who owned me came from somewhere north of Charleston county. I guess they did care for me some because when I was hit by a car they took me to the vets—only they never came back.

Anyway, I was in pretty bad shape, but the vets put me back together and then worried about what to do. After all, who wants a put-back-together dog who is way too thin? But they took really good care of me and always told me how sweet I was. (They were pretty sweet themselves—two surgeons and this little vet tech who was not exactly plump herself.)

One day a lady showed up at the clinic where I was living, where I was pretty happy, except that I had to spend a lot of time in the back room in a cage. Don't get me wrong. Everyone stopped by, took me out, and loved up on me as much as they could, but a clinic is always busy. The lady had been on a walk, and someone who knew her had heard that the clinic was looking for a home for a little white dog. She and her husband missed their dog, so everyone encouraged them to take a look. Instead, the dog looking for a home was me—pretty much the opposite of the plan.

She took me home, just to see. It was really scary in a way, but everyone (after doing double takes) looked me straight in the eyes and said, "Oh, yes!" So I stayed. And I meant to stay. If they left the door to the porch open, I made them close it. Once you find your home, you don't give it up.

They named me Frieda (which means "peaceful" in German and is the name of the grandmother of one their friends) and set upon a plan to fatten me up. One of the best ways to do this was to let me eat oysters in the country. Yes, they took me to the country where I met my best dog friends, two Labs and a Border collie. And I was the boss. I love being the boss. In a very nice way, of course.

Halloween came and I had a pumpkin costume, because I can look scary if you don't look in my eyes right away. I learned to bark, to stamp my feet on the ground to make a point (particularly about leaving that porch door open), to ride in a boat, to make friends with the neighborhood cats (a very nice group), and to realize that I had my home.

Now, I'm no longer way too thin (occasionally I'm made to eat Science Lite although I'm never denied oysters in season), and don't mind being teased about being that "little white dog."

FRIEDA

SAMANTHA

As all the guidebooks will tell you, the best way to explore Charleston is on foot. This works for those of us with four feet as well as two. However, according to my walker, several rules do apply.

Number one: Wear a leash or be exceedingly well behaved. I have to stay on a leash. Her arguments are as follows. All white cars are not driven by friends of mine and, therefore, may not know to stop. Some people don't want you to show them that you just found the nearest puddle. Running free is for nearby islands and fields, not cities.

Number two: Obey the pooper-scooper law. She feels very strongly about this. When I was young and in turn had young walkers, she was always handing us bags. We didn't always use them. She always uses hers. My predecessor was once pooping on High Battery when a man in a white truck objected. She had a bag; he was the police chief—the famous one. She didn't get arrested, but she knows some people who need to have this experience.

Number three: Enjoy your walk. That's the easy part.

My very favorite walk is in the early morning. It gets

the day off to a good start. After all, unlike the editor of this book, most of us don't get to go to work with our people. Lots of dogs and their people are out. Some have tennis balls; some are joggers; some are even bike protectors. We walk and then we stop and then we repeat. There are so many things to smell and taste. People are rather messy, and while this is upsetting to realize, it does have its good points. If she's not paying close attention, I can find bait on the Battery or around Colonial Lake—this doesn't not mean there are goats in my family tree, just that I am a springer spaniel, a gourmand if you will. Sunday mornings on King or Market are good too. Even though the restaurateurs try, the smells alone are well worth investigation. No wonder people come to Charleston to dine.

We also get to see other friends. Some days the dolphins will swim along with us. The pelicans and the hawks hang out at Colonial Lake. They are allowed to fish in there. I'm not allowed to jump in after those flying fish. Life is so unfair.

Afternoon walks are nice. Sometimes friends join us or we stop to visit or we go to observe springer puppy play group. She thinks that is so cute. Now really, why would I want to wrestle with a bunch of young Turks and let them jump on me? The cat understands that we play by my rules; my person keeps trying to socialize me. I planned this life. Some days we go up King Street and visit shops; some are quite friendly, even with water bowls. We both really like to play sit-and-stay; then she goes in for a quick minute and all the tourists tell me how cute and well behaved I am. It's a great act, especially on Wildlife Weekend. Those people are great for our egos—she never tells them that I don't hunt.

Anyway, she takes me for lots of walks. In return, I

don't play with shoes, well, I try not to play with shoes. The only dark spot on the horizon is the occasional mention of the cat learning to walk on a leash. I'm planning on cutting a deal with the cat.

Explore Charleston. You'll love it.

SAMANTHA

[Samantha, a nine-year-old, liver-and-white springer spaniel who has recently taken up Agility, is best known for her smile and the ability to find puddles even during severe droughts. When not walking around Charleston, she keeps her person and the cat amused and has people over to admire her portrait, painted by Faith Cameron Semmes.—Emmye Johnston]

LOUIS ARMSTRONG ("LOUIE")

Dog Agility must be the fastest growing sport in America. I've never seen such a dedicated bunch of devotees. Maybe "devotees" is too grandiose a word for this group. They live and die for each forty-second encounter with the jumps and weaves and teeters under the judge's watchful scrutiny. I am the husband of a handler, so I try to enthuse over every five-hour drive to the next venue for a couple of forty-second races against the clock. But I must admit that the handler's enthusiasm rubs off on me, and I watch transfixed as dog after dog is entreated to run faster and faster to beat the clock and get a "Q." And when a dog gets a "Q" (that's a "qualification") all hands shriek in approbation. It's one sport where all competitors root for each other. (I'm not used to that; must be a female kind of sports psyche.)

Well, Louie Armstrong is a black miniature poodle. The handler thinks she's number one on Louie's hit parade, but he has often told me that I'm number one. (It doesn't pay to argue the point.) They have been competing, with some success, at Agility trials for four years, but not quite able to catch the Border collies, Aussies, and other streamlined breeds built for the sport.

Nevertheless, it's not whether you win or lose, but only whether you play the game, right?

Well, one trip to Asheville (only four hours) was most memorable. We were staying with friends, so I could go to the arena later than the usual 8 A.M. Over three hundred dogs were competing, and you're never quite sure when your dog should be warmed up for the first run. (Of course they shouldn't peak too early!) It's a little bit of mass confusion. Well, I arrived with our friends just in time to see Louie and handler proceeding through the course of fifteen obstacles very stylishly—a "Q" and a blue ribbon as well! Wow. Smooth as silk. Our friends were appropriately impressed. We would have broken out the champagne, but it might have been frowned upon; this is serious business.

After watching another fifty dogs run, our friends left, prior to Louie's next event. I wished handler and dog well (the high sign) as they got into the lineup for the next run. They looked ready. Timer's ready. Go!

After ambling over the first two jumps, Louie just stopped and looked around . . . then another jump and another stop in spite of the handler's plea. "Louie, let's go!" Then the dreaded judge's whistle. That means get out of the ring. Wow turned to woe. She picked up Louie and carried him from the ring, saying "good doggie," but thinking "bad doggie." The problem diagnosed? Louie was looking for me! I was the problem.

So, for the last event the handler decided that Louie must know my whereabouts. The arena in Fletcher, North Carolina, is a wonderful horse-show building, undercover, with seating rows graduated up from the ring all the way around the facility. The handler took me to a spot about seven rows up, right at the finish line for the next run. (This was a "Jumpers" event with jumps being the majority of the obstacles. Louie is a very good jumper; he never knocks down a bar. Poodles have those long back legs built for jumping. So we always expect fast times from him.) Louie saw where I was . . . he wouldn't have to look around for me.

Well, their time came. Handler and dog fast out of the gate . . . over . . . over . . . over . . . fourteen obstacles, like the dog I call "the fastest dog in Charleston County." Then the next-to-last jump . . . coming right toward me . . . he looked up, took a short cut . . . into the grandstand, up the steps, and into my lap! The onlookers were in hysterics. Everyone, but the handler standing in the middle of the ring, humiliated. Now when I go to Agility trials I must hide. l am dropped off (as much as a mile from the event), say farewell to Louie, hike to the event, and slink behind posts and bleachers till his last event is history, win or lose. It's a dog's life.

HUGH B. HANSON

Tann Mann ("The Man," "Tanny Mann," "Mannequin")

Tann Mann entered my world nearly three years ago, a time when there was a deep sadness in my heart. Having just put my beautiful buff cocker, Waco, to sleep after his heartbreaking bout with pancreatic cancer, I was grieving intensely. Returning home every day to an empty home suddenly stripped of the happy pitter-patter of puppy paws and a dog's unconditional companionship was excruciating. Finally I decided the only thing I could do was to get another dog.

I knew I wanted a cocker, but chose to go with a chocolate instead of a buff cocker, fearful that I would make unfair comparisons. I also wanted to find a highly reputable breeder in order to avoid health problems later on. An internet search yielded the results I was seeking. I uncovered a show-dog breeder located in Fayetteville, North Carolina, that specialized in chocolate cockers. She sent me a photograph of her tiny five-month-old puppy gazing up stoically with golden-brown eyes as big as saucers. His eyes spoke to my soul. I was instantly drawn to the much loved, but slightly wayward, dog that had not made the show cut and needed a good home as a pet.

When I arrived in Fayetteville a few days later to meet him, the breeder took me back to the kennel area that was filled with a sea of beautiful chocolate cocker puppies. The first thing the breeder asked me was if I knew which one of these was Tann Mann. I glanced rapidly around, and almost instantly my eyes locked with his. He had the same steady, soulful gaze I'd seen in his photo. "That's him," I said to the breeder, correctly identifying Tann Mann, and in that moment our destiny was sealed.

We bonded instantly. The quiet, calm dog with a sage nature and funny name came home with me the following day.

From the get-go he seemed to sense I needed him, and he showered me with quiet, steady devotion, unusual in a puppy and in a cocker. Since then we've become inseparable.

Tann Mann's the mascot of my tennis team, a lover of fluffy squeak toys and cottage cheese, and a fan of naps and long walks. He struts when he walks, but it's less about boastful pride than it is about pure happiness. He's walked every inch of the peninsula and takes extra enjoyment in spending moments snapping at the water at the bottom of the steps that drop into the harbor off of White Point Gardens and chasing squirrels.

But Tann Mann's absolute favorite activity is his weekly trip to the Ralph Johnson VA, where he visits his special hospital friends as a therapy dog. The minute I snap on his I.D. tag to his collar he knows he's going to work and he's out the gate running to help spread the special form of joy that only a dog can give to help the patients feel better.

The softness of his fur, the sweetness of his soul, and his wagging tail all contribute, but it's his lowered head and shamelessly intense gaze, the same one I saw that first day, that do the most good, I think. As one patient says nearly every time we visit, "It's those eyes."

HOLLY HERRICK

CLEO AND FLETCHER KAMMEYER ("CLEO" AND "FLAVA")

Hi there! My name is Cleopatra, but everyone calls me Cleo. I'm a very pretty long-hair Chihuahua. Even though I'm a little overweight, my mom says there is more to hug! I have a big sister and her name is Fletcher. She's an Irish setter and she is twelve and a half years old. I'm young and frisky because I'm only four, so I must protect Fletcher from other dogs because she has arthritis and stuff. The old girl has a hard time getting around, but my mom makes her walk a mile with her every day. She really loves that. I don't like to go for walks because it's just too hot. Some people say I'm a little prissy, but I'm really very strong.

Mom has us go to the groomers once a month. They are very nice. We also get to have a massage while we are there. How many dogs do you know who get to have a massage? It sure feels good and I go to sleep. Life is just great!

Every morning we get up and go to work. Our family owns Rug Masters. We greet the customers nicely. Fletcher is better with children than I am. Personally, I don't like little children. They scare me, so I bark at them. My bark is bigger than my bite. I wouldn't bite a flea—well, maybe a flea. We work very hard to earn our keep!

Our favorite food is beef jerky. Fletcher likes it more that I do. Mom mixes it with our regular dog food, if you can imagine that! She thinks she is fooling us, but we just eat the good stuff and leave the rest. Sometimes Mom gets aggravated with us, but we have her number! Fletcher and I like to take long naps when we're not working with the customers. It's a rigorous life, but someone has to do it.

We just love to go on rides in the car. It's fun sitting in the driver's seat with Mom and Dad. I pretend that I'm driving and speeding over that new Ravenel bridge. Flava likes to sit in the passenger seat. She looks funny when the wind makes her ears fly back.

As you can see, my parents take extra-special care of us. We also have two cats at home. They are fun to play hide-and-seek with.

I really don't know how we got to have this family, but I thank God every day for all the love we have. I see pictures of other dogs at my house that Mom and Dad have had. Mom says someday we will all meet in heaven. She really believes that. I'm sure she is right. I'm proud of my parents. They help with Pet Helpers and other animal rescue places. I know they have a soft place in their hearts for all creatures great and small.

At the end of the day I say to Fletcher, "Good job," and we go home to snuggle up with Mom and Dad, and then awake in the morning and go again. I hope we have made you smile because we are two very happy critters!

CLEO

BEA WARING

Laugh all you want at the runt of the litter. I was the little bitch no one wanted, except this man who missed his old Lab. He could never replace Jimbo because no creature could measure up—until I came along.

I don't know what you have heard, but we do not receive advance warning on new arrivals in heaven. Must have been fifteen years since Big D said good-bye at the vet's office, and then I heard his voice as he called out: "Come, Bea."

Big D found his wings on the first cool weather day in the Lowcountry. I jumped through the celestial field and zigged and zagged until I saw him with his arms open. I licked his face when he leaned down to pet me; he began to talk about what he called our perfect hunt. It had been the same sort of cool day.

It was early October when I went to Edisto with Big D, Momma, and Son. Cousins were everywhere and the sky was chamber of commerce blue. I could hear Gamecock football across the field, but only when the guns quieted. The barrels flashed in the sunlight, swinging at the go-here, go-there flight pattern of the mourning dove.

Big D was in the middle of this uncut soybean field, and Son was on the edge near a road where Momma sat twenty yards away in the shade of a live oak. She drank her iced tea and clapped when she could see a bird fall. All three laughed when we arrived at our parking place because they saw me, the runt, become quickly lost in the green rows that covered better than a football field.

I could see them drop, but sometimes I was finding a bird for Big D when Son would shoot. Son would call me and point; I would run rabbit style—my pounce, pounce, pounce dance of the field. Then, stop and wind . . . then wind again. Gotcha! All they had to do was point. Bet a bunch of blockhead Labs couldn't get under those bean bushes—ha!

The best I did was find three—one at a time; they were all blind retrieves because I was having a water break near the Ford station wagon when the biggest flock of the afternoon came at them. Big D folded a pair with his over-and-under, and Son took a single—but with three shots. Big D always did better with doves.

Big D grinned and would pet me and speak about his sweet girl and good girl. Thank you, thank you; I repaid the kind words by rubbing slobbery feather balls on his brush pants. It did not seem to bother him.

He bragged on the springer runt when we returned to the Big House. That did not mean that he shared his Frogmore stew. No, sir. He and Son found cold beer in a washtub and told the red-faced cousins about the runt that could find birds. Momma verified it to Chief Know It All, who spoke so highly of the walrus-like Lab at his feet.

More than twenty years had passed as Big D continued to recall that day; as he paused, I pushed my nose under his arm—the way I did when I saw guns loaded into the station wagon. I ran in circles and still he did nothing. I wanted him to know we could go again since anything good was possible in heaven. He shook his head and held up two fingers and pointed down.

This runt knew we would have to wait and prepare for the unknown day when our season to be made whole again would come. There is so much to do, including learning to be friends with the likes of that Lab Jimbo.

BEA

SPENSIR QUILLINAN

There are hot dogs, River Dogs, and Blue Dogs in Charleston. There is a Charleston Canine Club, and there is the basset hound brigade in the Christmas parade. The hotels are dog friendly, the banks dispense biscuits, and the art galleries boast canine art extraordinaire. This is the haven to which I have come. I reside on Tradd Street, just a few strides from the dog park. I have been delivered to this marvelous place of great smells (food, feline, and frond), wondrous sights (horse-drawn carriages, house construction, and horticultural havens), and soothing sounds (the bells of First Scott's, Sunday singsongs, and the call of my name). Spensir . . . I am called Spensir. I hale from California and am the result of grand breeding—Bear's Outlaw and Felina's Outlaw Cowgirl, the pick of the litter of yellow Labrador retrievers.

Although I celebrated my tenth birthday this past October 10, the praise is high for my handsome looks and fit physical stature. Other than my Nylabone and a biscuit, I enjoy rides from the beach house in Kiawah to our downtown pied-à-terre on Tradd.

Welcoming me to the neighborhood was an invita-

115

tion to Poppy Baker's Twelth Birthday, a true Southern occasion: many friends (two black Labs, golden retriever, long-haired dachshund, Jack Russell terrier, and a specialty breed guest), scrumptious treats (sausages, biscuits, and Frosty Paws), and of course Miss Poppy Baker, herself, dressed in pink with rosebuds. Although I am well trained, I am not too refined and I barked a little too loudly at the unknown guests. It took a while for me to settle, but settle I did . . . after everyone was gone. Another Frosty Paws, a nuzzle next to Miss Poppy in her Sherpa bed—yes . . . Charleston . . . I am finally home.

SPENSIR

SCOUT ROSS

I don't get it. My mommy and daddy ask me all the time if I realize how lucky I am. How am I supposed to know what that means? I mean I am smart and all, but "lucky" isn't a word I understand. I think it is a good thing. If you ask me, I think they are the lucky ones.

I wish it were that simple. I really want to know what it means to be a "lucky" dog. I am a Brittany and it is our nature to be inquisitive. Maybe you can help me figure out what it means to be lucky.

I guess it all started when my parents first came to get me. I was living at a place around Ridgeville, South Carolina. I had seven brothers who loved to torment me. Maybe I was lucky because I was the only girl. Don't worry. I am a tough gal. I held my own.

Maybe I was lucky because my parents adopted me. Apparently they had planned to adopt someone else, but everything fell through. My mommy was so sad that she made my daddy drive out the very same day to look at me and my brothers. At first he refused. He said that they would have to make an emotional decision . . . whatever that means. Anyway, it must have been love at first sight because they came to my place and I fell at my daddy's feet. I have been his little girl ever since.

117

It is funny. Supposedly I am a hunting breed, but I have never hunted, so I am not sure what I am missing. My parents call me a "family dog." I sleep in their bed . . . they take me to the Farmer's Market every Saturday morning . . . and my one-year-old sister lets me eat her food off her tray when she is finished. Is that what it means to be lucky?

Speaking of my sister Kate, I was not very happy when she came along. I was only a year old when she was born, and I had been the center of my parents' universe. Then one day this new creature came along and she made very strange noises. Sometimes it seems like Mommy and Daddy forgot about me. But don't worry, I am Scout Ross. I cannot be forgotten. I used to take Kate's pacifiers or blankets and run around the yard with them. I thought Mommy and Daddy would enjoy chasing after me, but apparently not! Even though I got into trouble lots and lots those early days, they still let me sleep in their room. Maybe that's lucky.

I am not sure if I will ever know what it means to be lucky, though I think I have a good idea. My mommy started working recently at the SPCA. I heard her telling my daddy about the poor cats and dogs that need a home. They don't have little sisters who pull their hair and throw their toys. They don't have mommies and daddies who take them to the dog park or let them sleep in their beds.

I guess I do feel pretty lucky to have the family I have and the life I have. I wouldn't trade it for anything. Well, maybe for that bird that I would like to catch at the end of my yard.

SCOUT

XZENA

I was headed toward the waterway to cool off one day when I noticed something moving in the high grass near the water. I stepped closer to investigate, and new sights and smells swirled all around me! My feet sank into soft mud. Crabs scurried in and out of the dirt. Something on my right moved, and fast! The scent of salty life from all directions nearly made me woozy. A great bird landed and another soared off—oh, so help me, I love birds.

I quickly lost myself. I burrowed in the mud, then splashed in water that filled holes as fast as I could dig them. I pawed at crabs, even chased a deer. I tasted the oyster shells as I bounded over them after the birds. The very spirit of the marsh seeped into me. I was a dog possessed. My only thought was to go deeper into the marsh, to wallow in the mud forever.

Suddenly I found myself standing outside the marsh on solid ground. Harshly awakened, the dream over. Layers of thick mud covered me. It was so heavy I couldn't move as fast as I did in the marsh. I had a hard time breathing. My face was puffy, and mud was packed in my nose, my cheeks, and even between my teeth. The mud began to dry, caking my eyes nearly shut. It slowly dawned on me that it hurt to walk. But I couldn't limp because something pained each leg. I was so muddy no one could see that each paw was shredded by the jagged edges of those decadent oyster shells.

But the worst was not being in the marsh. I had been in the marsh. Now I wasn't. The loss was horrible. I had been chewed up and spit out of paradise.

The good vet eventually found the oyster cuts in my paws after lots of washing. He then squeezed my swollen leg. Out from my cuts burst mud! Everyone was astonished but me. I knew I had the life of the marsh flowing through my veins.

That was my first and last stint in the marsh. But it still calls to me. Sometimes I hop on the seawall at the Battery and peer over. And every now and then, at low tide, I think about jumping into the soft, dark mud on the other side.

XZENA

ELLIE

I was born up North, but I like the Charleston heat—
except when it's still warm enough in January to get a
bath.

ELLIE

MAXIMILIAN ("MAX")

No clock needed. It's a bark and a bark—a doggy command to head to the park. As I walk in the door, Max bellows the command—it's canine time.

It's a daily ritual—keys jingling, paws scrambling, and a mad dash to the car. With a sixty-pound white snowball riding shotgun, we hit Broad Street heading for the park. It's a ride full of anxious barking, paws scratching at the dashboard, and a big black nose soaking up fresh air out the window.

This is Max's daily routine come five o'clock, and it's a life we wouldn't want any other way. Our three years together have been anything but boring. I think it was just meant to be that I got elected to be Max's caregiver. I distinctly remember that day in November 2001, when I was in my vet's office waiting to pick up the cremated remains of my childhood dog. I happened to look up on the billboard in his office and saw a couple of chubby poodle puppies advertised for sale. I called the number immediately, assuming there were no puppies left. To my surprise there were three.

All poofed up, but sitting pretty, it was Max who I picked right away. We bonded strongly and quickly.

He's tutored me through dental school, made me take a lot of walks, and made me smile when the world seemed gloomy. It's hard to imagine life without my best friend.

He's always been a road tripper too. Whether the top is up or down, Max rides shotgun—not afraid to sit up like a person for a better view. When his owner has left the car, he usually heads to the driver's seat—as if that will bring me back to the car faster.

Sometimes I can't help but laugh when I do a few double takes of the white poofball behind the wheel. One time I remember pulling into a drugstore on Folly Road with Max riding in the front passenger seat. An elderly woman gave me a puzzled look and said, "I thought that was a person in the front seat with a dog costume on." "That's a dog," I said, and just laughed.

KRISTIN MURPHY

GRACIE PETERS

My name is Gracie. I am a black-and-white Shih Tzu who came to live in this "Holy City" (as I've heard it called) at the tender age of five months. I was born in a very different place they call Florida with only two cats named Edward and Valero as companions. They say I was taken away from my real mother very early in life. Now I make my home with my adopted grandparents in Charleston. At first it was disastrous! They had not had a dog for a long time, and it took me months and months to train them.

We live in a house that used to be a carriage house (they say that it was built around 1759 or so) on a very grand street with church bells, ladies who make and sell baskets, horse-drawn carriages, and lots and lots of other dogs walking their masters and mistresses.

When I first came here, I thought we really should move to the next block into a "great house" by the name of "The Nathaniel Russell House." I kept pulling on my leash in that direction, hoping my adopted grandparents would take notice. The gardens were the best I'd ever seen, and the grass was so green and lush.

I longed to live there. But, alas, my adopted grandparents wouldn't even let me loose to play there, and we never moved there, so I suffered my first *big* disappointment in life.

Shortly after that, I discovered a small park not too far from our carriage house. Suddenly, at the back of the park, I saw a very strange man who didn't move. I barked and barked and stood on my hind legs, outraged over this intruder in *my* park who didn't even acknowledge my presence. My adopted grandmother said, "Gracie, this is called a bronze statue; it honors a great statesman and politician named James Byrnes." Well, I've learned to tolerate James Byrnes. After all, I guess *my* park is big enough to share.

Now I am eight years old and have become quite a sophisticated *city* dog. Life has settled into a lovely daily routine. I have adjusted to our small courtyard with its blue-stone floor, statuary, and various planters. I take my adopted grandparents on long and wonderful walks every day, come rain or shine. (Here I need to make a note of the fact—I do not like rain.) I've also discovered that I have four adopted cousins who live nearby on Water Street: Patrick, a Lhasa apso, and three Pekinese (Su Ling, Luci Lu, and Charlie Chang), all "Charleston Dogs."

They say that Charleston is a lot like a European city, whatever that is. All that I know is that this little Florida transplant thinks that Charleston is the *greatest* place on earth to live, and I wouldn't change a thing!

As a postscript to my story: I've come to think of my adopted grandparents as my *real* grandparents, and I love them very much!

GRACIE

DANNY DOG

My story begins as a very young, very lonely pup in search of a home. As soon as I saw the house, I knew it was the home I had been searching for. Up the drive I scampered and claimed it as my own. The keepers of the house must have been very impressed with me. They posted my picture all around the area and took me to visit surrounding houses. Of course a name had to be chosen for me. It happened the day the grandchild came for a visit. As I raced up to greet the little darling, my lady-keeper, almost under her breath, declared me to be "TheDam Dog." The young grandchild quickly repeated this title. It was then that My Lady decided the title to be a bit formal and declared my daily name should be "The Danny Dog," "Danny" for short. Realizing that I am considered royalty, I have declared My Lady should also be titled. Henceforth she will always be known as "MyDam Lady," "Madam" for short—she loves it!

After six years of pampering the family and doing all I could to make our home the place of bliss it was meant to be—enter Black Dog Kelsey—my life was about to change. She, too, had been abandoned and in search of home-and-hearth to call her own. She is what is known in the canine world as a "Leaper." She leaps tall fences with a single bound. She ventured out of our kingdom often and always brought back treasures to share. This ended the day she saved a young lad's life. This young lad was toddling near a backyard pond, and Kelsey sounded the "bark alarm" to alert the nearby adults. She raced forward in case she was needed to rescue the young lad from the cold dark water. Everyone was quite excited. When she realized the little fellow was no longer in danger, Kelsey raced home to share this story of courage and bravery with me. Very soon visitors arrived at our house. I'm sure they were here to relay their thanks for Kelsey's heroic deed. Soon after that, she was rewarded with a lovely blue collar, which was not only lovely, but was a very special collar that makes sounds whenever Kelsey nears our tall fences. She no longer leaves our grounds, seeming content to stay and race and play with me. We still get visits from neighboring dogs, and we always wag our tails and bark it up a bit. Kelsey has now made it her duty to rid our domain of any creature, real or imagined, living under the ground. This entails digging many holes, an activity that Madam does not seem to appreciate. I have been delegated the position of peacekeeper and happiness maker. I do this with licks, leaps, and nuzzles. I must say, I am quite good at my job. I know this because I get many smiles, many hugs, and many treats. Life is good, and I am very glad I found this family to love.

DANNY

ADMIRAL LORD NELSON V ("NELSON")

My name is Admiral Lord Nelson V, but I prefer just to be called "Nelson." And I am the fifth in a line of Old English sheepdogs that have served "admirably" in the Ron and Sandy Phillips household as it moved about and eventually to the French Quarter here in Charleston. Because my predecessors enjoyed the company of the Phillips and of their three sons, and because the sons eventually married some mighty pretty ladies, I have been allowed to enjoy a more expanded family that now includes six little rascals.

I will admit that I am very demanding of attention—from the time I wake up my buddy Ron by bounding onto his bed promptly at 7 A.M. (my initial demand is toasted, generously buttered English muffins) until it is my bedtime. My morning snack is then followed by a jaunt through the French Quarter to greet all the early risers, including the Market Street vendors who are setting up for the day. I have many people-friends in the French Quarter, and though I do not have a tail and for that reason am also referred to as a "Bob Tail," I do waggle my bottom quite vigorously when they hail me by my name.

I especially like to play retrieval with a tennis ball at certain fenced sites, which include the U.S. Custom House grounds, where I start to play in the morning about the time the U.S. and South Carolina flags are raised and then move to other preferred sites later in the day. I always carry my own tennis ball on these outings, and all the nice people who know me also know that I am anxious to play ball retrieval with them as well as with my buddies Sandy and Ron.

I am now six years old and, like my four predecessors, I am very good-natured and still tend to act like a puppy, which gives me a good excuse for jumping up and lying next to one of the Phillips family—and that may be either on a sofa, a stuffed chair, or a properly made bed, depending on which opportunity is most convenient. However, when it storms or my house companion Barney, who is a loud-mouthed macaw, starts squawking, I prefer to retire to the shower stall, where I stay until either the storm or the squawks subside.

I do not consider that my food preferences and good-natured habits are unusual when compared to most other canines. For example, I especially like steak and prime rib, including the bones. I admit, however, that I did on one occasion help myself to a large portion of very delicious meatloaf when I was yet to be offered such. And that was simply because I was able to obtain it directly from the kitchen counter when no one was looking. As a result, it just came sooner than later.

I want to wish world peace for everyone and also wish that all canines enjoy a good and fun-filled family life like mine.

NELSON

BOO-BOO

My name is Boo-Boo. I'm an English bulldog and very beautiful, if I do say so myself. Others say I'm not so beautiful. In fact, I've heard the word "ugly" used at times. Apparently some people can't recognize true beauty when they see it.

Even if some people don't agree I'm the prettiest thing they've ever seen, I do try to be beautiful on the inside. I try. But sometimes I seem to get in a lot of trouble. My owner—or my "momma" as she calls herself—is constantly reminding me to behave. I think I behave just fine, thank you, but my momma doesn't seem to agree.

I like to eat the rose bushes that my momma grows, the ones with the cute little thorns on them. The flowers taste good, but the thorns tickle my throat and make me cough and foam up. That always scares my momma. I also like to grunt and snore a lot when company is over, which I think is a bull dog's privilege, but which my momma says isn't ladylike.

My favorite activity is drooling. I'm a definite pro. In fact, I'm so good at it, my momma gets her carpets and walls cleaned every six weeks. I think she's so sweet to do that. It's like an artist getting a brand new canvas to paint on.

My momma had her walls cleaned and repainted last week. She left to do some errands and I was sitting there, all alone and a little bored. That wet paint smelled so good and those walls looked so shiny, I thought it would be fun to rub up against them and play. I rubbed around until I was pure white (I'm usually brown). Then I rolled around on the carpets a good bit until they were white, too. I was so proud of myself. I couldn't wait to show my momma!

When she came home, I didn't get the exact reaction I was expecting. Momma came through the door, dropped everything she was carrying, and opened her mouth like she was going to say something. But she said nothing. She just stood there, with her eyes kind of popping out of her head, like mine usually do.

Well, I won't go into the ugly details of what happened next (which involved a lot of baths for me), but needless to say, I survived my painting experience. I don't think I'll be trying that again anytime soon.

I know my momma absolutely adores me (who wouldn't?) and spoils me rotten, but there is one thing she still hasn't learned. If my momma would just recognize the fact that I am the boss, in capital letters, and that I rule the world, then life would be perfect. We're still working on this issue.

Momma rescued me from the pound, where they were about to "put me to sleep." She gives me everything I want and pets me and talks to me and has lots of birthday parties for me. It's a great life, even if she reminds me to behave once in a while. In fact, it's such a great life, I'll just let her keep thinking she's in charge, even though we all know I'm the real boss of her and everything.

BOO-BOO

[Painting by, and courtesy of, Lese Corrigan]

TASHI AND CHAI

I am the fortunate mom of two Border collies named Chai and Tashi. Chai's name came from the Indian word for tea, and Tashi means "auspicious" or "lucky" in Tibetan.

Both dogs were found on Petfinder.com, an internet site that lists dogs according to the breed-mix you are looking for using your zip code to list those closest to you first. Chai came into my life two days after my Border collie mix, Tiger, died at thirteen. I was devastated when Tiger died, and I started looking for another dog right away.

There was "Annie" (now Chai) in Columbia, and she was wearing Tiger's face! They looked so much alike, and when I got her home she even acted like Tiger. It was a perfect match. She was six months old at the time of adoption.

When Chai was one and a half, I decided she needed a sister and started searching for another tricolor puppy like her. I found "Beau" (now Tashi), who is certainly not a tri-girl, but a black-and-white boy. He was unbelievably cute and we went to Georgia to get him. He was four months old at the time of adoption.

Chai is a therapy dog that makes visits to the VA, MUSC, local schools, and nursing homes. A friend, Jane Hirsch, also is a therapy handler for Chai and takes her on many visits. Someone once asked me if I go to MUSC to do therapy, and I said, "No, but my dog does." That always gets quite a laugh from anyone listening.

Chai has quite a few tricks that she demonstrates at the visits along with doing a bit of agility and catching Frisbees if we are doing a visit to a school where we can be outside.

Tashi has passed his therapy evaluation, but is quite a vocal dog, telling everyone how much he loves him or her, and may have to wait to mature a bit before he does regular visits. His yips declaring his love tend to scare people who don't know he is saying I love you, soooo much. Tashi tends to be stuck in those terrible teenage years of dogs. Most of the time I refer to him as my juvenile delinquent, or JD for short. He is also known as "Plume Boy," because of his fluffy tail that he most often carries high over his back. He is certainly lucky that he is cute. It makes his silly behavior easily forgiven.

Both dogs passed their Canine Good Citizen test on the same night. I was a very proud mom that night.

You will see us at least two days a week at James Island County Park. I am the one standing there with a tennis racket hitting ball after ball that the dogs chase lickety-split and bring back to me to hit again and again and again. . . . Other days of the week we are at Palmetto Park, Alhambra Hall, or dabbling with agility in West Ashley.

People who see us always ask if they are brother and

sister. I reply that they are in that they both are my kids, but they are not related. Chai is now three and a half and Tashi is two and a half.

I work as a dog trainer for one of the local pet stores, so I am fortunate to be able to take both dogs to work as demo dogs—Chai as the "good" one and Tashi as a work in progress.

Border collies as a breed require a lot of devotion on the part of their parents to keep them busy and entertained. They were bred to run a hundred miles a day and herd sheep on the border between England and Scotland. Many end up in shelters and in rescue because they don't have enough to do and find things to do that are not acceptable to their human caretakers. They are wonderful dogs if you are committed to supplying them with the mental and physical activities they need.

ANGIE HALL

DOLLY

It was July 1, 1998, when we picked up Dolly, an adorable Maltese, from the home of her original mother and father. We were told she had been born two years prior, but were not given an exact date. Because we do not know her birthday, we celebrate it on July 1, which is the anniversary of her coming to live with us. With her sweet spirit and loving personality, Dolly immediately became part of the family. She was invited to all the social gatherings and endeared herself to children and adults alike.

Dolly lived with us for seven years before her father had the idea to share her with the world. He says, "Whenever my wife and I take Dolly out in public, she receives a lot of attention. Weighing just over four pounds, people are amazed at how small she is and how cute she looks. She has an under-bite that makes her little tongue hang out of her mouth. We call it the 'cute factor.' The more her tongue hangs out, the higher the cute factor number, with a ten being the highest value."

With the idea to share Dolly with the world, we started the first Dolly book, *A Dolly Fashion Show*. We had collected numerous outfits for her over the years, which included dresses, sweaters, hats, shoes, T-shirts, scarves, and Halloween costumes. Many of her clothes were made by her mother. Dolly's outfits were used to create the premise for the book. In the book Dolly has a favorite outfit for each month of the year. Margaret W. Atwood, a professional local photographer, was commissioned to shoot the pictures for the book.

Dolly's father says, "The book is just good wholesome entertainment for children of all ages. We live in a time when the family pet is no longer just a pet, but an actual member of the family. They give as much love as they receive and more." We donate a large portion of the proceeds to the John Ancrum SPCA and to Pet Helpers Rescue & Adoption Center. We believe it is important to do this so other little "boys and girls" like Dolly will have the chance to find loving homes.

Dolly is also a registered therapy dog. She and her mother take the time on Sunday afternoons to visit Oak Haven, which is an assisted living facility located in West Ashley. There people know Dolly by name and look forward to her visits. As a part of the Woof to Read Program, Dolly and her mother go to Ashley River Creative Arts Elementary on Tuesdays. There the children with reading difficulties read to Dolly in a non-threatening, nonjudgmental environment. Dolly's mother has seen children improve their reading skills in just a matter of weeks. Dolly believes in giving back to the community and spreading joy to all those around her any way she can. For more information on Dolly or her book, visit Dolly's website: DollyBooks.com

DERRICK HORRES

JOSE ("BEANER")

I must tell you about my little guy Jose. He is a four-pound Chihuahua who thinks that he is a Great Dane. This little treasure came to me by accident, and he is the joy of my life.

I was at a gathering years ago. My father had lost his little Chihuahua, and a lady had a Chihuahua at this gathering. I asked her where did she got her little dog, and she said she had one at home I could have if I would just come get him. I went to her house the next day. As I drove up to her house there were two little dogs up on the couch. I saw Jose and I said to myself, Please let that be the one. It was. The lady called him a true Southern name, "Bubba"; I changed his name to "Jose" that day.

Jose has had many, many adventures, which I have to tell you about. He now travels with me in my purse, he has fathered eleven puppies, and his charisma wins over each and every person he comes in contact with.

He was run over by a car. My father found him in the middle of the road on the yellow line, cars flying by on a Friday night. Jose made it.

Once when he was lost, I called the radio station, a

man heard my announcement, and called my father. The man said Jose was running with a pack of dogs. The man could not believe his eyes when he saw this little dog leading a pack of six or seven dogs. He brought Jose home the next day. The man did not know any better, but he had given Jose a pound of raw hamburger meat.

One time Jose ate kitty litter. He couldn't go to the bathroom for a week. He never touched kitty litter again.

Jose was lost several times, but because I had his name and phone number on his tag, he has always been returned to me.

He grew up with his big brother Jessie, who was a pit bull mix. One day Jessie bit Jose all the way down his body. Jose made it.

We lived on fifty-two acres. I always had to watch and make sure that a local hawk that always watched Jose did not try to pick him up.

Once my father took Jose for a ride. Some French fries fell in the back floorboard. Jose went to get them. My dad's car door flew open when he turned at an intersection. When my father got home, we could not find Jose, so we went back to where the door had come open. Jose had fallen out of the car at the intersection, but there he was at the fruit stand, some lady holding him.

Last year a German shepherd came into our yard and jumped on Jose. Jose went inside to his bed. Four hours later, when I was working in the yard, I noticed that my other little dog, Kita, had been barking for a long time inside the house. She even turned a chair over. So I went inside. I looked everywhere for Jose. I finally found him. When I picked him up, all of his insides fell out in my hands. For four hours he had been like this. Needless to say, I rushed him once again to the emergency room. He made it.

Jose is truly a treasure. He remembers places where he has been. He is a comedian. I also have dressed him up in little clothes made for him. His body color is also very rare—red. I have never seen any other Chihuahua this color. He is a true Southern gentleman who has fought many battles and won most. Jose loves all people. He climbs in your lap and you do not even notice how he got there. He has brought joy to me and my family and to many other people as well.

LETA MCDANIEL

OTIS
("OTIE," "OTEATHA," "O," "OTE-MAN")
AND
SHASTA
("SHASTEATHA," "SHASTA LEE,"
"SHASTA-BO-DASTA")

It's nice to be able to go back home every now and then, to check on the family and see what's new in the hood. Some dogs prefer to make the trip during warmer months, especially those who lived in the Northern states. Shasta and I did our stint in the Chicago area for eight years. Talk about cold! Snow would reach up to my belly more days than not, and I'm a big Chocolate. Being three legged, Shasta had her complaints with it, but doggone if she didn't love swimming in Lake Michigan (when it wasn't frozen, that is). She'd go just about anywhere for a ball, and she'd *gladly* go in the water. No, Shasta and I are Southern Dawgs . . . born in the Carolinas . . . so South is where we're headed.

We've picked Christmas time to visit this year. Christmas in Charleston can be gloriously mild, sprinkled with a few frosty days, just to get you in the spirit. We originally moved there back in 1999. I'll never forget how excited we all were to be near the ocean. Shasta was starting to fail then. I always felt sorry for going to the beach without her, but I couldn't stand to miss the opportunity. When the folks grabbed their chairs and sunscreen, I'd be the first to hit the door. I was generally the first one back as well, sandy and wet, full of stories for Shasta. Both of us will never forget the time our family couldn't stand leaving her behind, so she got to ride to the dunes in the kids' wagon, and then they carried her out to the surf. What joy! I fell all over myself, trying to give her little love nips along the way. (Frankly, she still says that my lack of emotional control is what she likes and dislikes about me.) Now that I think about it, that was the last time she saw the waves.

Our present destination is Home Sweet Home on the Harbor. The smells (and taste) of pluff mud still thrill us both. It's great to see the folks. The other three dogs always cut up when we arrive—jumping, and laughing, and barking. I'm amazed the folks don't find it curious.

Boy oh boy, we've got a dock now! Look in the house: there's still dog hair in the corners and toenail scratches on the wooden floors. Not much has changed. Our collars still hang on the mantle in the breakfast room, next to our Christmas stockings that the folks continue to put out. My gosh, those people miss us as much as we miss them. That's why we get to come back.

It's hard to believe we've been gone at all. I guess Shasta died four years ago? I finally gave up the ghost about this time last year, there on the best rug in the house by the big bay window. I didn't want to go, but Shasta came to say it was time. My hips had given out, my hearing was shot, and my eyesight was gone. When my heart finally stopped, there wasn't a dry eye in the house. But hey, look at me now, fit as a fiddle . . . and

Shasta, on those four legs, can give anybody a run for his money!

Well, let's take one more turn around the homestead, noses to the ground, tails in the air, and then we'll be on our way. Sure it's tough leaving, but we'll be back. And I'll let you in on a little secret: it also helps to know that heaven is a lot like home in Charleston.

OTIS

MR. EMMETT
("EMBO")

I feel like I won the lottery! I am such a lucky little dog.
Let me start at the beginning.

You see, I am a salt-and-pepper-colored miniature
schnauzer named Mr. Emmett. (You might have heard
about me since there is a book called *Stroll with Mr.
Emmett.*) I lived the first nine years of my life with my
bachelor father. We had a very exciting life. Sometimes
I wished that our house was quieter or that we would
go to bed earlier. Sleeping is a favorite hobby of mine!
I love my poppa very much. I would often go on the
job with him during the day. When the weather was too
hot in Charleston, I would have to stay home by myself
all day. I would sleep and look out the window at the
beautiful garden and the river. I was always happy when
Poppa would arrive home.

One day my life changed. The lady a few doors away
retired from her teaching position. For some reason she
took a liking to me. This was very strange, since I used
to bark at her all the time. All of a sudden we became
best friends. She takes me on long walks all around the
city. She takes me to the park. We do errands together.

144

Now I do not have to spend my days alone. Sometimes I even do sleep-overs. I have two homes in Charleston.

I must admit that there are times when I do not know which home to go to. One week Mrs. L was having work done on her house. There were workers in and out, and they all loved me, even when I barked at them. Well, one day I was supposed to stay at my poppa's house because Mr. and Mrs. L went away for the day. The workers came to the house and I followed them in. When they left, I stayed. Naturally the workers thought that I belonged there. Well, my poppa had the entire neighborhood looking for me. Everyone was so upset. I was very comfortable on my bed in Mrs. L's house. I wondered why people were yelling outside. They were all very loud and interfering with my sleep. I could not understand why no one came to take me outside. Mrs. L never stayed away all day! After all, I might need a walk.

Finally Mr. and Mrs. L came home. The neighbors ran to their car to tell them that something had happened to me. Mrs. L immediately went over to my poppa's house. Mr. L came into his house. Boy, was I happy to see him. If you think I was happy, you should have seen my poppa and Mrs. L. They both were crying and hugging me. I will never understand what the big deal was! I had had a very peaceful day! They did not find out until later how I managed to get into the house.

What a day that was! Everyone in the neighborhood laughed at the excitement that I had caused. I certainly was not excited. I was too busy sleeping.

EMBO

Z
("Zed")

Z is my name. They pronounce my name Zed because I am English, a distinctly "English" cocker spaniel, not to be confused with the "American" kind. . . . I was born in New England like my sister, Lucy, whom you already know. But my English characteristics go no further than my name, my heritage, and my birthplace, for I am anything but proper.

How so, you may wonder? It is *my* mission in life to do everything *Wrong*. A bit of a bungler, ol' sport, maybe "W" would be a better name for me. Lucy, my sister, is my nemesis; she's perfect and a star. She apparently was named after a Lucille Ball, another famous red-haired female. Lucy is featured on the internet, is now an editor of this book, and spends the day at the Dog Art Dealer with Mom, lying on her back begging dog-art connoisseurs for scratches. Now me, I get too restless and nervous to go very far from home. Mom cannot get much done when I jump onto her lap, begging to go home. No, my domain is Lamboll Street.

On little Lamboll Street I am calm, watch over the property, and look for mischievous deeds to do and for food to eat. And watch out, I'm fast, ol' sport! A bagel can disappear in half a second, as well as that vitamin pill you dropped.

The most exciting twenty-four hours of my life was an Easter Sunday. My people had a family visiting, and Sunday morning there were three baskets of candy that the children carelessly or generously left out for me to enjoy. Mom didn't know about my inconspicuous consumption, but that night my tummy was aching—the aluminum foil is a little hard to digest—so she let me out very late at night. I forgot to tell you that I'm also a talented escape artist. Oh temptation! A gate had been accidentally left open. I realized this was an opportunity to play "Dog on the Run" and slipped out while Mom was absorbed reading her newspaper.

Bow wow, I got to run up and down the narrow streets in Charleston, and it was garbage day! So many tasty, smelly garbage cans. I was in heaven—except heaven decided to open up and it started to pour. I do not like getting wet, ol' sport. Maybe I was being punished for being so bad. Was this purgatory? Well, I sloshed on and on, then . . . bow wow . . . I smelled the most delicious meal ever. I understand the President even came here for lunch, barbeque, and lots of bones! Sticky Paws or something like that. Well, this was heaven, divine, scrum delicious, then, oh no, . . . down the street comes one of those humans in the blue suits with the baseball bats and pop guns.

What! He put me in the back of his car, which was screened in like the cage I stay in when my people savor my beloved food. This is not heaven. Who was this stranger? I was sopping wet and wanted more barbeque and don't like strangers. Then . . . oh yes, ol' sport, it was the familiar smell of Lamboll Street—and there was Mom with a big warm towel, wrapping me up and carrying me into our warm and dry house. Maybe home isn't so bad after all. Maybe Lucy doesn't have it all wrong. But it won't be long before I forget, ol' sport, and get back in the thick of it . . . in trouble again.

ZED

LILY SOMMONS

You know you own a vizsla if you're wearing one on your head. Someone said that to me years after I had brought Lily home. She was the sweetest dog in the litter. I got to meet her just three weeks after *whimper* she entered this world. I knew she was the one for me when—after I picked her up, she peed on me. From then on she was known *whimper* as "purple" for the rickrack tied around her neck. That's a true story, and, yes, I've been wearing her on my head *whimper* . . . ever since.

What is wrong with you? *Green beans.* Green beans? *You snuck green beans into my dinner again, didn't you?* I'm trying to write a nice little story about you. Do you think you could just eat around the green beans? *I don't particularly like green beans.* Yeah, I get it, but do you have to keep crying about it? *I really like potatoes.* We didn't have potatoes tonight. *Well, I really like them.* Okay, I like them too. When I make potatoes again, I will be sure to make an extra helping for you. *Are you joking me?* No, a whole potatoe just for you. But right now you'll have to be quiet, so I can get this story finished. *Mashed or roasted?* Umm, mashed. *Mashed is good. I like mashed.* Okay, Lily, mashed it is. Now go lie down!

She's been the easiest dog to train. She'll do anything for me, or for a small cache of food. She can even fetch me a root beer out of the fridge. *Are you telling them the whole "peed on you story"?* Ergh, I told you to lie down. *Let me see what you are writing.* You can't read. *What's this word p-o-t-a-t-o-e?* It's potatoe, the food you like so much. *Well, you misspelled it. It's "potato" without an "e."* Go lay down. *Do you me lie down?*

As I was saying, she's a real peach. Doesn't do anything wrong, ever. Sleeps quietly at the end of the bed (she never ever snores). She loves the children, even the one who pulls on her ears. The cats can cuddle next to her, and she won't even flinch. She doesn't dig holes and she stays in the yard all day. And if you were to leave a delicious birthday cake right on the kitchen counter where she could get it, she would never. She doesn't bark at the mailman, milkman, meterman, delivery-man, or cableman. She never gets fleas and she doesn't stink. She gives kisses and her breath smells like roses.

Do you honestly think they will believe that? *They'll think you wrote it.* I'll delete it. *No, don't.* Perhaps I should tell them the real story. *The one where I saved you from the burning house?* Uh no. *The story about how we were stranded in the woods and I searched everywhere in the freshly fallen snow to find a rabbit for us to eat?* Yeah, that one, where you started the fire with the wet branches. . . . *I love that story.*

RIC SOMMONS AND LILY

LIBBY LOU SINGER

I knew something terrible was happening, but being just one lonely chubby Jack Russell, I was not sure really what was going on. I had lived in an apartment in Georgia for the first eight years of my life. Then a baby came along, and a couple of months later I took a long trip. I was not sure why, but definitely found out soon enough.

We stopped and got out of the car and talked to a couple of ladies. He put my special food dish, which said "DOG" on the side of it in blue, inside the car along with my toys. I sure hoped that I would get some new toys and a new dish. Before I knew it I was placed in my carrier in the back of that Jeep! The back of the Jeep shut down, and that was the last I ever saw of him. I was very frightened.

It was another long trip until we got to the lady's house. The nice lady took me, my dog dish, my toys, and my carrier inside her house. I wanted to hide inside my carrier because that was the only security I knew. What was this? To my surprise there were already two other dogs living there. Their names were Corky and Princess. They looked nothing alike, but later I found out that they were sisters. The lady had some great treats for us. She stroked me, hugged me, and told me that she thought I was a very pretty dog, and sure did "love my groceries"—like herself, she said.

And that night I did *not* get put in my carrier. I got to sleep wherever I wanted. Unbelievable—Corky and Princess slept in the bed, right on the pillows. The nice lady patted the bed and invited me up. And you know what, she did not just call me "Libby" (which was my name), but she called me "Libby Lou." I was surprised and not at all sure if I liked that new addition to my name. I crawled under the covers and slept right by her legs, up close and snugly.

About two months later we moved out to the country, and there were even more dogs: four more Jack Russells, the two terrier mixes (Corky and Princess), two Border collies, and a very, very old hound dog. It is great. There is a doggie door, and we all come in and go out as we please. We chase birds and lizards, howl when the train goes by, dig holes . . . and almost never get into any trouble.

After coming to live here in Charleston, I have learned from Jack (the very, very old hound dog) that people get a dog and keep it forever—because dogs are part of the family. So I am really part of a family forever now. And my new mom says that she loves me more than any dog she has ever had. And me and my new mom still really love our groceries. And we all still get to sleep wherever we want—under the covers, right up close and snugly!

LIBBY LOU

SAXON ("THE HAWG")

It all started in 1996, when I was born on the Fourth of July near Charleston. I am a big-boned girl, red and white. I have lots of freckles and am very beautiful.

Life was uncertain at first: my first mom could not take care of me. My real mom found me when I was nine weeks old, and we have been together ever since.

I wasn't always queen. For a while there was just my mom and me. When I was two, my mom got me the little basset brother I always wanted: Bailey is red and white like me. His second birthday was the same week we got him. I love my little brother so much! He had to stay in the crate at first so I wouldn't hurt him.

Now that I have someone (besides my mom) to rule, I am a real queen.

It isn't easy being queen. The hardest part is training people. It's easier if you have one person trained: that person can help teach others the right way to do things. I worked hard to train my mom, and then I got a dad for Bailey and me. I prefer to train Dad myself, because Mom tells him "big-boned girls have to watch their weight" and other nonsense. My dad shares my love of pizza, and I have trained him to feed the "pizza bones" to the basset hounds: queen first, of course. Did I mention my nickname is "The Hawg"?

I do a little to help other basset hounds. I allow certain bassets waiting for a home of their own to stay at my house. They are called foster dogs and I rule them all.

I am busy sleeping most of the day (unless it's time to eat), so here is how I have things set up. Bailey is the Foster Supervisor; he handles the details. Mom and Dad work to earn money to take care of me and the other bassets. In their spare time they help Carolina Basset Hound Rescue (I try to keep them occupied).

My objective is to impress upon each foster that I am the queen. I have different teaching methods. One is positioning myself across the hall with the foster dog on one end. The foster dog can walk past the queen only when I decide the time is right. Most fosters learn quickly, but sometimes they forget to be respectful and I have to meet with the offender individually. They learn that the queen eats first, sits where she wants to sit, and has the best toys.

Even a queen can have misfortune. When I was five I got a disease called primary glaucoma and it hurt! Some doctors tried to help, but I lost sight in one eye, then in the other, and had to have surgery *two times*. I am very brave and had to help my mom, who is not so brave. It's not hard for me to rule as queen, even though I am blind, because as a basset hound I am a *very* good smeller (that's not the same as smelling good).

If you ever have the chance to meet me, you can pet me. I am humble. I'll like you best if you have a snack to share.

SAXON

154

SUMMER ("BUBBA," "LITTLE BEAR")

My name is Summer, and my mommy told me to tell you a little about my life as a dog. I get confused a lot because sometimes she calls me a dog and other times it's "Boo-boo Bear" or "Bubba."

All I know is I get to live a lot like she does. I have my own pillow and sleep on the right side of the bed. I get a little cold sometimes, so I make sure I snuggle up to Mommy. She says I take up a lot of the bed, but I really need to sleep on my back and stretch out my legs.

I have lots of friends who love me. I walk to Miss Sue's house every day and scratch on her door. Sometimes I have to cry really loud so she can hear me. I get bones and a belly rub at each visit. Sometimes it is really hot, so I just run across the street to Miss Denise's house. She only has healthy treats.

Truman lives next door and we play every day. He is a lot bigger than me, but I love to run after him and chew on his ears. I might be small, but I sure am fast. His mommy puts up a gate to block off certain areas in the house. I'm not sure why she does, but I have really learned to jump high.

Mommy is a teacher and sometimes I get to go to

school with her. I get lots of belly rubs at school, and all the kids there are the same size as me. My feelings get hurt because I can't eat with the kids in the cafeteria. I don't know why. I know how to sit in a chair. I even know how to stay, and I am not a picky eater.

I like to swim in the water. Every day my mommy walks me in a different location in the Charleston area and lets me play in the water. Except one time she got really mad because I jumped in a lake that was filled with ducks. I thought they looked like fun new friends, but my mommy didn't think so.

My favorite thing is to ride in the car sitting in Mommy's lap with my head out the window. She always tries to put pillows in the seat next to her. I don't know who she expects to sit there. Sometimes people stare at me and laugh. I don't get it! Is my hair sticking up?

Sometimes my skin gets itchy and I have to see the doctor. They sure do like to rub my belly and look at my ears. There are lots of fun friends there to play with. Sometimes it gets really loud with all the dogs talking. Mommy tells me to stop barking. I don't know what that means, so I just keep on talking.

I love to see my mommy when she comes home from work. She is so happy to see me! Of course that's when she starts using all her nicknames for me. Well, that's my story of my life as a dog or maybe a bear. All I know is I sure do like it.

BUBBA

CeeDee ("CD")

I got CeeDee from the puppy farm. Well, that's what I always say. Actually it was a little town in South Carolina called Hartsville, on a beautiful, giant piece of farmland with a house, two golden retrievers, and lots of brand new puppies. It also included a very nice family looking for good homes for all the puppies. Hartsville really was the perfect name since CeeDee has such a big heart.

From the moment I saw her, peeking at me from behind the bushes, she was the most beautiful little girl in the world—a small, very fuzzy blond, five-week-old puppy, with the biggest, brightest smile that everyone could feel.

I was living in Florence, South Carolina. I was the radio girl, always moving for these crazy radio DJ jobs that barely paid enough to live. One afternoon I was sitting on the edge of the bed in my room when it came to me. I had the most sudden intense desire to get a dog. My family had always had a dog. We were dog people. I had owned a dog (Annie) part-time when I first moved out of my parents' house. The boyfriend, then husband, was not a dog person. Annie ended up back at my mother's house. Needless to say, the relationship with the dog lasted longer than the one with the man. She lived to be fourteen.

I was now a single mom, and my son lived with me. His eleventh birthday was coming up. It was time . . . to have a dog. I was drawn to pick up the newspaper, and in it was an ad I picked out immediately: two sets of puppies, born to sister golden retrievers, free to good homes. I asked my friend Sherry, a girl I worked with, to ride with me to Hartsville. My son was visiting his dad in Charleston for the weekend, so I jumped in the car and drove forty minutes or so to Hartsville, to fall in love.

It was never Sherry's intention to actually get a puppy. I, on the other hand, being an honest person, knew how I would react, but tried to stay open to the fact that I needed to get the right puppy for my family's atmosphere. As in all relationships, it needs to be the right fit.

I had the directions for the house. I'd never been to Hartsville. The countryside was so beautiful. After driving up to the front of the house, Sherry and I got out of my Jeep and headed to the back, to the sound of puppies. There, in a huge fenced-in yard, with lots of trees, shade, and flower bushes, were fourteen beautiful strawberry blond puppies. I fell in love.

The owner of the property and her children were so friendly and kind. I remember the young girl playing with the puppies, and they were trying to decide which two puppies, of the two litters, to keep. As we talked, the puppies ran around. One set of puppies was a golden-chow mix. The other, a golden-spaniel mix. Sherry decided on the golden-chow mix and scooped her puppy up. I knew immediately I wanted one of the golden-spaniel mixes. Both litters had been born on the same day, January 26, 1995. They were a few days away from being six weeks old, and the owner wanted us to make our choices and come back. But we were in love.

At least I was, with at least three of the puppies. Their faces were incredible. The golden-spaniel mix made their bodies very soft, with small floppy ears, and golden curls, ringlets even. I was trying to make my choice when the young girl said she had picked the two she wanted to keep as she held them in her arms. Suddenly one hopped out and ran behind the bushes. That's when I picked her up. I scooped her from behind the bush, where she was trying to hide, and held her up to look into her big brown eyes. And then it happened, she smiled at me. From that moment on, my life would never be the same.

The little girl said she wanted to keep that one, but I knew—this little one was the one for me, and I had to take her home, right then. We met the puppies' mothers—two gorgeous full-blooded golden retrievers, very red with blond highlights. She told me the father was a full-blooded Boykin spaniel. I didn't know at the time, but that made CeeDee a drop.

She looked just like her mother, reddish and golden, like a small golden retriever, with a dash of spaniel. What was mesmerizing was her face. The sweetest face in the whole world, with big brown eyes and a mouth that "smiled." The funny thing was, I wasn't the only one who noticed this. Complete strangers noticed these things too! I would take her to the soccer field with my son, to the grocery store, and to work, when I was out hosting a live radio remote. Even to the mall, back home in Charleston. I hated to be away from her. My mom would even take her to the mall. People would swarm around us, wanting to see the pretty puppy. And she . . . would smile at them. Everyone would ooh and aah. I felt like I was carrying gold in my arms. And I really was.

That first night home it was just me and CeeDee. It had been a while since I had a puppy. It really was just like having a brand new little baby. I had forgotten about half of the many items I would need for her. On the way home she rode with me in my Jeep and immediately became a car dog. She sat beside me on the seat, and then behind the seat, under the seat, and then back on the seat again. And then, she smiled at me.

We went home to settle down in our new life and for CeeDee to settle into my shoes, in which she became very cozy, and in which she just about fit. To this day CeeDee loves to lie with her nose in my shoes, especially house shoes.

DENA LAMBRAKOS

MAGDALA ROSE ("MAGGIE ROSE")

I've had this dog almost two years now. People tell me that after two years things will get better. I'm still hopeful.

My initial idea was that when I retire, Maggie Rose and I would be a team—a therapy dog team, bringing comfort and happiness to those we visited. After the first four months, it became evident that the only one who was going to need therapy was me.

I waited for her for two months with great anticipation. Finally I would have a big dog that would go on long, leisurely walks with me, that would lie quietly by my side when I got home from work, and that everyone in the neighborhood would love. *What was I thinking?*

The first clue that things might not go as planned was when I read her papers. Breed: Giant Schnauzer; Color: Black; Dam: You Only Live Once; Sire: Airline Pilot.

Early on, and being a working dog, she developed an intense interest in exploring a variety of career opportunities. A talent for excavating and landscaping emerged overnight following the installation of a sprinkler system in our yard. Artistic tendencies were displayed through furniture redesign and fashion modeling. Equipped with a gleaming set of teeth rivaling the hardness and edge of any lathe tool, she could gnaw a nondescript piece of furniture into a rococo designer original in a matter of minutes. She took great pride in her sense of fashion by wearing delicate garments in unusual ways and delighted in modeling her newest creations for whomever happened to be visiting.

Devoted to helping Miss Maggie become the best that she can be, we have exposed her to a variety of experiences. During this time she has instilled great character and a humility of spirit in my husband and me as we have endured the embarrassment of her having to repeat beginner obedience class not once, but three times.

We did experience a glimmer of hope at our last rally class. As we were waiting our turn, Maggie Rose ambled over to a door on the side of the gym and pawed it. I told the person next to me, "I believe Maggie needs to go out." She looked at me and said, "Well, I guess so." She points to the sign by the door—"Restroom." Maggie Rose can read!

As we are nearing the end of the two-year, trial-by-fire mark, my husband and I would like to express our sincere thanks to the numerous dog trainers and dog wranglers who have encouraged us and contributed to the raisin' of Miss Maggie Rose. Any evidence of misbehavior, downright bullheadedness, tearing loose, and overexuberance is solely the responsibility of the owners and should not reflect negatively on those whose services we have sought. Glimpses of goodness, endearing antics, and gifts of gentleness (even though short-lived) reassure us that our beloved Miss Maggie Rose is just on the verge of "turning good."

BOBBIE LINDSTROM

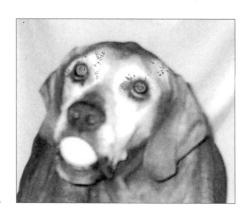

PIPER

My name is Piper and I am a Hungarian vizsla. I've been with my owners a long time and they really "treat" me well. A perfect example of this is how they enjoy my hobby. I discovered years ago that if I retrieve certain things, my owners get excited and give me "treats." The all-time favorite items I like to rescue are those little white round balls. Let me explain how this got started. Years ago my owner would pretend to throw a ball into the thick weeds around the golf course that we lived near, and I would find a ball just to please him and, of course, get a "treat." Now all he has to do is say "Ball" and off I go. Sometimes I would even dig down several inches to find them—those are really dirty, but still worth a "treat." My hobby was put on hold when we moved from my happy hunting grounds.

Several years later a friend of ours, Ken Berger, who is a sports writer for the *Post and Courier*, heard about my hobby and wrote about it. At that time, I've been told, I had retrieved about four hundred balls. It was really nice to be famous for a short time. Several humans wanted to borrow me when they went golfing, but I only fetch for my human.

163

But we have a happy ending here. After being away from my hobby for eight years, we just moved next to that same golf course. Even though I'm a lot older, with legs that tremble and eyes that are a little cloudy, I can still find those balls. Maybe not as quickly, but my nose never fails me. I now have a partner, Lady. She is much younger and I am teaching her everything I know. The only problem is she is faster than I am and finds some of the balls before I do.

My partner and I now have about nine hundred balls, and my human is starting to play golf. Even though I'm slowing down, we will continue to make my owner happy.

I'm tired now, so I think I'll take a little nap. Happy golfing—keep losing those little white balls!

PIPER

Tippa Sullivan Wood ("Tippa")

Wagener Terrace has been Tippa's neighborhood home for nearly ten years. It was on Dunnemann Avenue where she started her running career, joining her new owners on a daily trek to a nearby track. For the next five years she became a regular and media favorite at the Hampton Park Fun Run Series, annual Turkey Day Runs, and Charleston Reindeer Runs. Tippa, now long in tooth, continues to exercise daily with a walk to Brittlebank Park accompanied by her canine companion, Wendy.

Tippa's first introduction to a regular running routine was at The Citadel track. As a puppy she scampered in every left-right-backward-forward direction, but she was a quick study and soon learned track etiquette. There, on Tuesday mornings, she would join the best runners of Charleston. Her really tough competitors included Tom Mather and Bob Schlau. Other regulars were Thad Bell and Charles.

In the summer of 1997 Tippa joined the friendly crowd of runners for her first in a long series of Hampton Park Fun Runs. These 5K races—on really, really hot or really, really cold Saturday mornings—were the highlight of Tippa's workless week. To say she was an enthusiastic runner is an understatement. Dave Eason, the park's race director with a flare for teasing, was the target of Tippa's ferocious intensity, especially when Dave's mouth fired "bang," which, as everyone knew, "was louder than a gun." For several years Tippa received "A" report cards for attendance, but she was no match for her friend Rex McNeely, who ran seventy-two consecutive runs between 1997 and 2000. During her Fun Run days, Tippa made many friends, including Sandra Conradi, Karen Emmons, Lyn Hammond, Barbara O'Grady, Laura Osborne, Margaret Wright, Jerry Gunter, Don Miller, and Dr. Paul, to name just a few. Tippa received a special dog trophy in recognition of her Fun Run participation and was mentioned in David Quick's Running column in the *Post and Courier* in July 2000.

It takes a special pet to tolerate an owner's compulsion for dressing them up for special occasions. Tippa is no exception. In order to run in special races, like the Knights of Columbus Turkey Day Run or MUSC Children's Hospital Reindeer Run, Tippa would don the appropriate garb. These races earned her a featured photo in the *Post and Courier*, a star appearance on the TV nightly news, trophies from the Reindeer Run, and of course many "blessings" as a Turkey Day trotter.

Tippa's racing days are over. With the exception of periodic yips, she seems very content to sit on the sidelines at The Citadel track and wait for her owners to finish exercising. Her canine companion Wendy leads the way these days. Wendy is a showstopper herself, having halted President Bush's motorcade during his visit to The Citadel in Fall 2001 while she and a sibling—both on the lam—crossed Mary Murray Boulevard. Wendy joined Tippa's family shortly thereafter, after being rescued by a caring neighbor and her namesake.

JOANN SULLIVAN WOOD

CHELSEA ("FIELDSTONE'S MIDNIGHT STAR," "THE VELVET MOUSE")

My name is Chelsea (a.k.a. Fieldstone's Midnight Star). But at my age I'm now known by some as "The Velvet Mouse." The person who gave me that moniker has a real sense of irony. She says that now that I'm almost entirely deaf, with a rich soft coat and arthritis that would cripple a horse, I have the demure personality of a field mouse, including that soft "mousy" fur! Still, I have a strong heart, a fierce sense of loyalty, and I still love to swim.

But the truth is I wasn't always like this. I was once "Chelsea the Destroyer of All Things Made of Paper," "Chelsea the Canine Soprano Who Accompanies Fire Trucks and Kids Singing Happy Birthday," and "Chelsea the She Devil of Cape Cod Bay," courageous swimmer of the oceans no matter what the weather. I was also "Chelsea the Dear One" to little kids who would see me with my father carrying his lunch bag in my mouth (got up to being able to carry a twelve-ounce soda plus a humongous sandwich because he was a big eater several years ago). I was "Chelsea the Protector of the Back Yard" and "Chelsea the Guardian of the Family Food Supply." My fierce dislike of mailmen had me being

168

quarantined for two weeks several years ago because of a mailman who had no sense of humor. For heaven's sake, it was just a little pinch—not a bite. Not really.

But now I'd like to think of myself as "Chelsea the Languid Southern Girl." In Charleston, where I now live, there is something in the air and it's wonderfully sweet. Dad calls it Tea Olives, sometimes it's jasmine. Sometimes it's fried chicken wafting around like some kind of seductive zephyr. But the combination thrills me no end. Still I enjoy the languid nature of the weather, the occasional visits to the beach for a swim, and the walks around town that I now take with the assistance of a cute little red wagon.

Imagine, if you will, the ability to manipulate humans with a look. Hence, the wagon. My mom, dad, and baby sister (also in this book) go for a walk. Before we go, I glance at the red wagon. A *loooong haaaard* glance. Dad puts a pillow in it and off we go. As walking gets more difficult, I glance at it again and then just stop in my tracks. Bingo! He's got the message and I'm up in the wagon. The rest of the "walk" is me in the wagon feeling like Cleopatra gliding along in "Chelsea's Chariot."

These little wagon rides are especially nice on Marion Square during the Farmer's Market. Mom has finally figured out that I will share my movable bed with her groceries while we're there. So, I get the ride and a few little nibbles of stuff here and there.

But these days I sleep a lot. Sometimes in a nice little sunspot in the living room; sometimes on my big old pillow next to the television. But sometimes, when the weather gets real cold, I get to sleep up on the bed under the blankets. Mostly, though, on the cool floor in the summer. God made something very special when

169

he made heart-pine floors. In fact he must have had all dogs in mind.

Charleston is my home now, and there are no more hard winters for me—just walks on the beach, rides in the wagon, and warm days and nights to dream of "Chelsea the Destroyer of All Things Paper," "Chelsea the She Devil of Cape Cod Bay," or, what the heck, "The Velvet Mouse."

CHELSEA

BOB

We see them everywhere, on the side of country roads and in the city streets all over this great land—dogs living like their ancestors have since the dawn of time. Some look like they belong out there scavenging off the largess of our society. Others just don't fit. You wonder, Why are they not curled up at someone's feet or in a warm lap?

One crisp November afternoon I drove by a resident roadside scavenger on Interstate 26 near Woodruff, South Carolina. At first I kept going, citing a number of excuses to myself. First of all, I really need to stop by and see a particular client before they leave for the day, and second, he is probably just a beagle separated from his pack and I have never had any success getting "those types" to come along with me. Something made me pull over and back up on the shoulder. Armed with a "Cookies and Cream" Cliff bar and a lot of love, I set out to get this little guy into my car.

As I got closer I saw that he wasn't a typical pack dog, and he definitely didn't belong out there. His coat was so matted and caked with mud that it had formed an impermeable suit of armor. If his armor wasn't enough to keep away would-be predators, the stench that accompanied him would surely do the trick. Almost immediately I started calling him "Bob." Maybe it was the "dread locks"? As his personality emerged, it began to fit more and more. The next day we journeyed back to Charleston and straight to my friend and groomer, Betsy Arrington, to get his suit of armor removed. After a couple days he emerged an emotional and behavioral basket case, but he was clean and on the road to recovery.

I tried to give him away several times, but it was hard to find someone who would and could deal with the baggage that was attached. Very quickly I grew attached, and he made it clear that I was his. In the past year Bob has gone from a thirteen-pound skeleton that was scared of everything—and made it known by piddling and snapping with regularity—to a pretty well adjusted and confident twenty-five-pound bundle of energy. I don't know what breed he is and don't like to guess or dwell on it. For all I know he is an angel, as he came along at just the right time to help me through the loss of my canine companion of twelve years. He is loyal to a fault and has an endless supply of affection to share. Rescuing or adopting a dog may not be for everyone and isn't something that one should dive into without serious preparation and consideration. Try fostering a dog or cat, however, and you might find that you are the one that gets adopted!

MARC WELSH

DUNDALK
HE'S A LOVER
("PADDY")

"Is today *the* day?" Every day I wake up, this thought stirs in my brain. It's my favorite day of the year. My birthday, you say? Nope. Christmas, you might guess? Nope. I guess I best back up and tell you a little something about myself. You see, my name is Paddy (short for Patrick), and I'm a four-year-old soft-coated wheaten terrier, living in downtown Charleston with my pack members, the Wallaces. "Wheaties," as we are known, are originally from Ireland, and we still love cool weather and the feeling of wind blowing through our long honey-colored hair.

But, enough of this! Let me tell you about my favorite day—St. Patrick's Day, of course. That's when my pack members, the aforementioned Wallaces and my sister Reagan's pack, the Carders, throw the best party in Charleston, and it's always on St. Patrick's Day. It's held at our local dog park, and all the the wheaten terriers in the area are invited. It's a sight to behold! Twenty some Wheaties celebrating in our own inimitable way by jumping up and pawing each other's faces. See, that's our secret code! We have party favors of green bandanas and "greenies" to eat, and many of the guests are my relatives. You might say it's a family reunion—trust me, it's swell!

My cousins Grady, Riley, and Cooper all come after a session at the groomers. Wow, they look so spiffed up! Sully and Murphy and Grady's pack sister, Millie, always show up and sometimes bring treats for the human pack members. They sure seem to enjoy themselves too.

I have to share a special secret. A new guest this year was Chelsea, a Wheatie from England. She has a spot in my heart, as I love that European flare she gives off. But I forgot the most important guest of honor at our celebration! That would be Hobbs of the Williams pack. You see, Hobbs is fourteen years old, and he's so wise and so sophisticated. We young ones think he's just the cat's meow (no pun intended). My pack members met Hobbs and the Williamses six years ago on King Street, and that wonderful meeting sealed the deal. That is why I came to Charleston, and I owe him a lot!

Well, that's all for now. It's time for me to go for a walk and charm all the tourists in town (just kidding). But who knows? This may be the start of a new wheaten pack in Charleston. Sure hope so!

PADDY

LION LEE
WAITZMAN
("LEE")

My first memories as a puppy were living at the SPCA in Delaware, where I was adopted by an organization called Canine Partners for Life, where I was given a new name and a home, and started training myself as a service dog. It took one year to learn all of the special tasks that I would need to know in order to help my future dad. In the spring of 1991 I first met my team member who would soon be my new dad. My dad, a man named Jim, met me as I was leading a mini-parade at a CPL fund-raising event. Balloons were flying high above my head as I pranced proudly in a circle around the park in Centerville, Pennsylvania. I was still in training, but the director wanted us to meet each other. I overheard my dad say that he was very pleased with my intelligence, but he would not be fully introduced to my unique personality until team training began in the spring of 1992.

My dad and his mom trekked down to CPL for our three-week training session. It was a challenging experience that included many retrieval and assistance tasks that prepared us for our new life ahead. After training, home we went where we jumped right into public life as

175

reading tutors for elementary school children. The kids related very well with me and Dad. Dad says that I am a great icebreaker when meeting folks that are not familiar with wheelchairs. It makes me feel proud that I can help my dad when he gets himself into a bind or when he just needs someone to talk to.

In 1993 we moved to Mt. Pleasant, South Carolina, where we attended Trident Technical College for three years. Everyone knew who I was, while sometimes forgetting my dad's name. After all, Dad keeps telling me that I am the star of the show. Dad and I received a standing ovation at the commencement ceremony, and I didn't want to leave the stage. Off to the working world we went shortly after college and have been performing as a team until this past year, when I was retired as a working service dog.

Twelve wonderful years as a working team have passed by so quickly. Dad always tells me that he couldn't have done it without me. Our journey together has taken us to many interesting places. From our inexperienced beginnings to me sauntering back with my award ribbon in mouth as South Carolina Veterinarians Hall of Fame inductee of 1999 to our rewarding working career. Dad tells me that I am his shoulder, confidant, and all-round good buddy.

Retirement means more time for me to rest my bones at home and share with my grandma and grandpa as well as my neighborhood dog buddies Dixie, Spooky, and Casey. I may have slowed down some, but my commitment to my dad will never waiver. Dad says that a well-deserved rest is surely owed to me, but we all know that my enthusiasm to assist my dad will never diminish.

LEE

COVINGTON'S SURFER BOY ("SURFER BOY")

My name is Surfer Boy, and I live in Mt. Pleasant with my mom and my little brother, Splash. I am a Boykin spaniel, the state dog of South Carolina. Splash is a Cavalier King Charles spaniel. I have the best life that a dog could have. My mom is the president of the Low Country Dog Agility Club. That means that I have lots of doggie friends and people friends. The dogs are really cool, and all of the people always have treats in their pockets. We all get together and play this game called "dog agility." We learn to jump, run fast, climb over stuff, run through tunnels, and weave through poles. It takes a while to master the game. The hard part is doing them in the order that the judge tells you. Sometimes it is harder for the people than the dogs. My mom is one of those types of people. She is always getting lost on the course. I am very forgiving of her mistakes. I guess I am going to have to learn how to read the numbers. We will keep practicing. She needs more practice than me.

Once you start to get good at the game, you can enter dog shows. I love to go to dog shows. I think they call them a dog show because you get to show off. When we go to dog shows, all of my friends go too. We stay in hotels and eat really good treats. My mom takes all of my special stuff. The whole weekend centers on making me happy.

She packs the car full of my stuff, and she only gets one little spot for her suitcase. I have a special tent, a shade cloth to keep me cool, at least two crates, my travel bag, as well as my little brother and his stuff. There are also lots of vendors at dog shows selling all of my favorite things. I especially like the food and the toys they sell. Splash likes to hang out in the puppy pen.

My mom talks to her friends about the best way for me to run the course. Then she and her friends go out and walk around the course with their imaginary dogs and try to decide the best way to tell us how to run the course. She always has a plan. You know what they say about the best-made plans . . . oh well. There are times, however, when the two of us just click, and when that happens, it is party time! I get these really pretty ribbons. They are different colors, depending upon how good you do. My mom has a wall in our house that she hangs them on. It makes me look very special.

I do believe that my mom would still love me just as much if I never did another jump. She still takes me for swims and throws my tennis ball. She loves my little brother and he is still pretty stupid. I should not say that, he is just starting to learn how to play the game.

SURFER BOY

FUZZY PROZAC TURNER ("FUZZY")

It was a few summers ago that my mum explained to me that we were moving to Charleston. My mum assured me that I would love it; she said it was the only place in America where she would even consider living. Mum had just returned from a visit home and wanted to be near her aging parents. She explained to me that she didn't want to get that "phone call" in the middle of the night; she wanted to spend time with her parents in their final years.

The arrangements would take some time, and our move date was set for mid-January. We loved Ireland with all our hearts and would miss our soggy green home. But we were also very excited. Mum dreamed of taking her dad and me to the beach. I wondered what the sheep would smell like.

It was on a wet and windy December evening that my mum got the phone call. Her dad was ill. The flight was appalling, but Mum was there to greet me. Despite the protestations of the man in the uniform, Mum opened my kennel and immediately led me outside. Even though it was an airport, it smelled gorgeous! Could it really be winter? Oh the pure sensual joy of it.

I peeeeeed and peed some more. Then I drank some water and was ready to begin my new life. There was so much I wanted to do, to smell, to explore. Oh, the fragrance, the warmth, the sound, I felt drunk.

As soon as we were in the car, my mum buried her head in my thick collie neck fur ("Collie Kleenex" as she calls it) and wept and wept. I think she cried more than I peed. Mum's dear old dad was dead. My excitement and joy were muted as my heart shattered for her. I licked her tears, her hands, her face. Oh, Mum, I love you so much, don't cry. When you cry my world crumbles.

Hmm, speaking of crumbling worlds, was Mum's grief so profound that I was expected to drive? I am a Border collie and able for any task, but where was the steering wheel? Ah, whew, Mum is driving. (Sometimes I still jump into the wrong side.)

Time passed and Mum slowly healed. Our medicine was the streets of Charleston. In the evenings, when it was cool enough for my Irish blood, we would wander her beloved alleys and lanes. Stolls Alley to Church Street, Longitude Lane back to East Bay. Down along the Battery. I loved the old, uneven slates, the deep crevices where cool, damp, ancient smells lurked.

I never knew the world contained such flowers, such pure bliss for the nose. And then there's the One, the Smell. I can die at any moment and it is okay. I have filled my nose, my lungs, and my soul with pluff mud. The smell of life, of teeming life in gorgeous marshes. The smell of Charleston.

But best of all, the medicine that healed us both was the warmth and kindness of the Charlestonians. I have never been so fussed over and petted as I have here. Why they even have doggie water fountains!

It's coming on Christmas again. Mum smiles most of the time now, and our adventures never stop. I am the happiest of Border collies. All is well.

But sometimes at night, as I drift off on my porch to the sounds I have grown to love, sometimes there is one niggling thought—Where are the sheep?

FUZZY

SEDGEWICK
EMMERTON
TORRENCE

Another year had passed and suddenly it was puppy season in Charleston again. That time from mid-summer to early fall when it seems as though the streets are filled with college kids and families alike, all toting leashes with a bouncing Labrador, terrier, or Yorkie puppy on the other end. That feeling began to creep over me, as it does every year when faced with this same phenomena—I wanted a puppy. Sure, my four-year-old dog, Scout, was great, but nothing compares to a puppy. So I started looking for a new doggie in newspapers, through breeders, and on the internet. I knew I wanted something small, and I knew I wanted a girl (they're just so much more fun, what with the pink sweaters and all). After a few weeks of research that seemed to be getting me nowhere, and prices seeming exorbitant for creatures that were little more than moving cotton balls, I started to think about adoption. My heart still set on a puppy, I thought that perhaps I could find one at a shelter. But, alas, all shelter dogs seemed to be some sort of Lab or retriever mix, a fine sort, I'm sure, but completely overdone, not to mention far too gargantuan for my current living situation. I wanted a small dog, but one that would stand out.

Finally I stumbled upon the perfect little creature on an adoption website. He was a six-and-a-half pound Pomeranian, full grown at somewhere between two and three years old. He was not the puppy I had been looking for, nor was he a girl, but he was just right. I drove an hour out to Goose Creek to visit my potential new dog and fell in love instantly. I was told he had likely been abused, as was evident by his excessive shyness and some injuries with which he came to the shelter. He had shorn hair, as his coat, which his previous owner had failed to brush, had become matted down to the skin. He had been used as a breeding dog, and had endured terrible hardships, including being constantly crated and recently treated for heartworm (which is both lengthy and painful, and requires being confined to a crate for months). He was emaciated and flea ridden. He did not trust me. This was fine with me, for as I had been told he might not yet be house-trained, I didn't particularly trust him either. We were perfect for each other; he just didn't realize it yet.

During the whole ride home, he glared at me. I set up his bed in the kitchen, another one in the bedroom, and another on the porch, littering each with a plethora of toys and chewy sticks. I fed him dinner and unsuccessfully tried to teach him to sit. That night, I picked him up and tried to place him in the bed, allowing him to sleep with me, but he quickly jumped off and opted to sleep under the bed instead, so I let him. A week passed with nearly the same daily routine. I would do everything I could think of to win his trust, with him glaring at me all the while. In the meantime, always the English major, I named him Sedgewick, after a woman who wrote several provocative explications on a handful of famous texts. If you should happen to know anything about her work, it would fit to say that my dog enjoys the company of other males. Then one night, as I lay in bed reading, I heard the distinctive jingle of dog tags, and looked up to see that Sedge had climbed up to be with me. The glare was gone, and we've been inseparable ever since.

The similarities between us continue to grow: both of us get cold easily, both of us require infinite amounts of hair care, and neither of us particularly trusts men. Sedgewick is now a therapy dog, and goes with me on visits to nursing homes and hospitals several days a week. He is also involved in a reading program, Woof to Read, and goes to a local elementary school two days a week to listen to children who are learning to read. The little dog who was so shy becomes increasingly social every day and has finally learned to trust again.

LEIGH TORRENCE

ALEXA TOMLIN

I am a dog bred to hunt, though nothing could persuade me to chase a fox or tree a raccoon. I am not of the Boykin family nor a ball-obsessed retriever, nor am I one of those loquacious terriers that appears to be multiplying as fast as the vermin they are bred to exterminate.

I simply am not interested in noisy and manic occupations. After all, when one can catch her prey as silently and quickly as an oyster is swallowed, there is no need for excessive panting.

My background is quite a bit more impressive than that of my Charleston peers. Temple drawings of my ancestors in Turkey date to 6000 B.C. Appropriate, don't you think, that I live where dead relatives are every bit as important as those who are alive?

I'm an S.O.B.. When I first heard that, I argued that I was a daughter, thus D.O.B., but was then informed that this is an acronym for "South of Broad." That's where the elite live, and certainly I am that. An elegant appearance is second only to an elongated pedigree in this neighborhood.

I have to confess, however, that my existence was not always so charmed. I was born on a farm in Arizona, and shipped to Florida to make my debut as a racer. Right away I knew it was beneath me. The food was substandard, and life merely consisted of sleeping in a crate and exercising with far too many other dogs in a dusty field absolutely devoid of amenities.

There were training periods in which we were encouraged to chase a ragged ball of hair. Anyone with a brain could tell that it was never alive. I heard rumors that those who did not win in the races would be offered early retirement in a private home. This was not known to be true, but I took my chances. I won one spectacular race to preserve my self-esteem, then slacked off and never repeated my stellar performance.

The risk paid off. I was pulled from the masses and adopted by The Mistress in Charleston, an ideal location for one with my distinguished heritage and elegant bearing. Each day we stroll through the shady old streets to the Battery, where I socialize with congenial companions.

Poodles know their place. Their heritage is not nearly as distinguished as mine, but they compensate with a most agreeable intelligence. Corgis likewise. They are cheerful and wise, although, for me, their stature renders communication a bit awkward. Cockers are quite amiable as well. They seem to have gotten past a primitive need to constantly "fetch" and have become pleasantly civilized.

Life is good here for a greyhound, but don't let the word get around. I wouldn't want to become . . . well, common, you know. But I suppose I need not worry. That is what blue blood is all about, is it not? If one is born to aristocracy, she remains forever an aristocrat.

"Cream always rises to the top," The Mistress says. I'm lapping it up.

ALEXA TOMLIN

NEMO WANNAMAKER ("NEMO")

My name is Nemo Wannamaker, soon to be Nemo Wannamaker-Chafik, as my mom tells me we are getting a new dad. My two young years have been quite a whirlwind, and because of that I'm used to things like new dads, so I won't complain.

I was born somewhere in the upstate of South Carolina, but my former parents decided they didn't love me. I had some defects, I'm told. In fact, one of Mom's friends still calls me "Lemon," cause when I came to live in downtown Charleston with Mom, I had to have two (expensive, I'm told) surgeries, and I had to wear this *stupid* lampshade thing around my head for weeks.

Anyway, my lemon-like qualities must have been what landed me in the pound where Mom found me. One day they took us out of the pound to this store for lots of people to see us. It was fun—all of these people kept coming up to my cage and sticking their hands inside. I just smiled and wagged my tail (it could churn butter it goes so fast, some say!), but most of them just kept walking by. Finally, at the end of the day, Mom came in and she picked me. I sure was lucky. She took me to great doctors, and now life couldn't be better.

I've got a great pad in the Historic District. It's cool living down here. I love to stick my nose through everyone's wrought iron fence on our walks. It's fun to see the beautiful gardens inside, but once in a while I get in trouble. One day a Jack Russell came flying out of nowhere behind the fence and latched onto my nose! I guess that was supposed to be my lesson—that I shouldn't be nosing around other people's property. I also love Charleston because there are interesting creatures like horses, bats, and roaches to chase. Roaches are my favorite. I pounce on them and crush them with my paws. Someone should give me a job with the exterminator. I am highly educated, you know; I've graduated from Obedience, Agility, and Acting and Tricks classes!

I've also got a beach house over in Hilton Head. I hear that's where all the snooty dogs and Yankies go, but I like it. I can run after birds for miles on the beach. Mom always yells at me to come back, but I don't turn around til all the birds are gone. It's funny to watch her get so frantic, as if I'd run away from this great deal.

Over at Hilton Head I've also two cousins named Sport and Maggie, who are black-and-white spotted just like me, and also came from the pound. In fact, Mom almost didn't adopt me because "she didn't want another black-and-white dog." Can you believe the prejudice that exists in this world? Anyway, I sure am glad that she picked me and that I get to live here. Life is good in Charleston.

NEMO

LILY

She wasn't much to look at. As a contact for English setter rescue, I was accustomed to seeing homeless setters in various states of neglect, but Lily, as her intake tag read, didn't seem to be neglected. Although she was skinny, with a thin white coat, she appeared to be healthy. Her orange spots were few and far between; I guess that's how she got her name. She seemed small and fragile as I looked at her through the kennel bars. Her fur was short, not at all what I had come to expect from a setter. I didn't think too much of her, and was already wondering what to do about her.

My "job" was to positively identify English setters and then start the wheels turning in the rescue process. I lived in an apartment, and as a single teacher didn't feel that I could commit to having a dog of my own. Dogs were too much responsibility. Identification and transport were all I could, or would, do for our rescue group. I led her outside and tried to assess her personality. She was very birdie, but didn't seem very interested in me. *Unusually* calm, almost boring were the thoughts going through my mind as I held her leash and wondered what to do. I knew I couldn't take her. She didn't fit into my plan. I always thought I would get a puppy, train her to be "wonderdog," and live happily ever after. A one-year-old, gun-shy, never-been-in-the-house dog was *not* what I had planned. No, she would have to go back in the kennel. I would do what I could to get her out of the SPCA before her time ran out, but that would be the extent of my involvement.

And then she did it. On the way back to the kennel, this quiet, "boring" dog, who wasn't much to look at, who had never been in a house, rolled over on her back in the middle of the cacophony of barks, yips, growls, and howls and "asked" for a belly rub. She literally rolled over on my feet, stopping me in my tracks, as if to let me know that there was more to her than met the eye. I bent over, rubbed her belly, and then it was over. My life as a single person ended. I filled in the paperwork, signed my name, and she was mine. One of the hardest things I ever did was put her back in the kennel. She couldn't go home until she was spayed; she had to spend one more night at the shelter.

I left in a state of panic. What had I done? This was a commitment that would last for the next ten to fifteen years. What if there was something terrible that I had missed? What if she didn't get along with my cat? What if (the scariest thought of all) I actually allowed myself to get attached, or to even love her? What if she broke my heart?

I should have trusted Lily. She knew what she was doing. She and I have been together now for seven years.

She has earned a Companion Dog obedience title, the
A. K. C. Canine Good Citizen certificate, and is a registered therapy dog. She even spends the day at school
with me, but only if she wants to. She has her little
quirks (eating toilet paper right off the roll), and it turns
out she is afraid of my cat. But she and I are a team. And
I am a little less reluctant to make a commitment. And
she looks a whole lot prettier.

BECKY STRONG

GIZMO SETTLE

When I was about four weeks old, I had my first encounter with my adoptive mother, Rebecca. It wasn't
anything special, though, because she couldn't touch or
hold me. They said I might get sick. It must have killed
her because I was just so darn cute. About two weeks
later she came again to hold me for the first time. I was
very shy because I was only used to fur balls and an occasional meeting with my owner. I was also very jealous
because my brother was out, too. I kept wondering why
she had both of us out. Couldn't she see I was definitely
the cuter one? But I guess she didn't want to make my
brother feel bad. She is just so sweet.

Two weeks later Rebecca came back to take me
home. I would officially be called Gizmo. That's when
I really opened up! I was jumping and running around
to show her how excited I was! Just when I was about to
burst, I saw it. The moving terror—or in human terms,
a car. I slunk into my mom's arms and started to shake
to show her that I did not want to get into that thing! I
realized that I was being a baby, which I was surely not,
so I tried to be strong. But that just wasn't working, so I

slunk back into my mom's arms. Hey, I can't be strong all the time.

Once I got settled into my new home, met my older housemate, Belle, the golden retriever, had my first vet appointment (very scary), and sniffed till I was content, my mom decided I should have my very first walk in the yard. It was heaven! The grass was so soft and I even had my own personal jungle. They had monkey grass in their yard and it was taller than me! I felt like a tiger! I would crouch down really low so she couldn't see me and then I would pounce. When I got tired, she took me back inside to see if I would take a nap. As if I could go all night long if I wanted to, but I wanted to make her happy so I went to my new bed, and just as I closed my eyes I got a glimpse of what looked like one of my siblings. Had they adopted one of them too? I had to see who it was. When I looked at its face, I saw that it only had one eye and it was very fat. It was a cat! We had one at my old home and he was great fun! When I went to sniff you-know-where to say "hello," the cat smacked me on the nose. Thank goodness she had no front claws. I later learned that this sassy cat was named Wink. I thought it was a very clever name. As I was asking myself why Wink didn't want me to say hello, another cat sneaked up behind me. This cat was much leaner and looked really scared. I decided I would try to say hello to her, but the same thing happened, and her smack was much harder. I could already tell she wasn't going to be nearly as much fun as Wink. I backed off and heard my mom say that Dusty wouldn't hurt me, so I called that cat "Dusty." After I kept trying to be nice and they kept smacking me, I thought that maybe a smack to them meant friendship, but the smacks kept getting harder, so I ruled that option out.

As I grew older and more mature, my mom started to teach me tricks. First she taught me the basics like sit, stay, and come. I was pretty good at learning them, if I do say so myself, and I really liked the treats. Then she went on to the tricks with which she would show me off to people, including fetch, up, and bounce. Personally, bouncing is my favorite and I think it's my mom's too. I'm like the Energizer Bunny. I keep bouncing and bouncing and bouncing. I can always get a good laugh out of Rebecca by doing it.

I can't tell a story without mentioning one thing. It is my favorite thing in the world. What is it, you ask? The "zooms." I get the zooms when I just don't want to take a nap and I want to go crazy. I get that look in my eye—the one that says you will never catch me—and then I am off! I run until I can't run anymore. Sometimes my mom thinks it's funny unless we are outside. Then she gets annoyed. That's part of the reason why I love it so much.

I'm six months old now and I have gotten wiser. I know that the cats do not want me to sniff you-know-where, I shouldn't do a trick unless I hear the word "treat," and if I have the zooms, don't try to stop me.

Keep zooming,

GIZMO

TIFFANY

She arrived in the world after much anticipation and anxious waiting by her mom. She was a tiny little thing, all smooth, black and tan. She came home to much love and tender protection to grow into a very vocal type- A girl to be heard. "Is she one of those little barking dogs," asks the sales clerk at the pet store? Little did we know.

She is a Southern belle, full of prissiness in her step and attentive to life around her. Tiffany—a little Yorkshire terrier with almost the smarts of a person and a desire to do anything she needs to do to protect her humans. Maybe from the great big squeaky ironing board or quite possibly from the range hood towering over the stove, much to the pleasure of her mother it is a welcome relief from one more mundane chore. Dry cleaning and the launderer are mighty welcome. She would rather see her master coming through the door bringing in the clothes all wrapped in plastic than to hear the awful squeak of that metal platform with legs.

Tiffany is on constant guard to any unusual noise other than the normal sounds of the day or night. A 4:30 A.M. smoke alarm failure with its tiny intermittent beep will have everyone up and out of the bed so that the alarm may be silenced and Tiffany will be calmed and stop her barking. She has done her job and is proud. Now everyone can go back to sleep.

The next day can bring a variety of ear raisers. Could it be the garbage truck stealing our things again or maybe UPS making a surprise delivery? Upon listening a bit longer, the conclusion is made. With a poke of her head into the obtrusive black tube, giving a round of barks, and one bite for the stamp of approval, the excitement yields a package addressed to Miss Tiffany. It is a special box of cookies meant just for her.

Don't even tell her that we have to go on a diet. She doesn't like the word and even less the meaning. I couldn't agree more. The mention of a squirrel in the backyard will have her licking her lips if only in a dream, watching the little critters dance and play from the patio door. Oh, for the windows of heaven to drop an endless supply of treats or maybe even a squirrel. Yum!

And boy does she like her treats. It's a reward for a job well done—a treat for having eaten her treat, she would say—"I think I deserve another."

Any minute of any day is the perfect opportunity for a game of ball. Throw it as fast as you can. Tiffany will be there as quick as a flash of lightning, a blur of black-and-tan hair flowing in the wind, waiting to retrieve and bring it back to be thrown just one more time, just once more, and again.

Ask if she wants to go bye-bye and the barking begins. It's a splendid day for travel with a bark at every click of the turn signal and the deceleration of the gas pedal. Where are we going this time and who are we going to see? Could it be Grandmamma or maybe Daisy and Pebbles? Not the veterinarian, oh please! No, it's only a day at the doggie spa, for which she is grateful.

She is the follower, foot for foot as not to miss a thing. All day long she is there close beside to comfort, to protect, to guard. She gives so much love and steals our hearts away with her sweet little brown eyes and nub of a tail. She is our Tiffany, our precious treasure.

DEBORAH TILSON

CAMILLA

My name is Camilla. Camilla is a pretty name. I have a pretty face, a pretty sable coat, a pretty purple collar with daisies on it (matching leash, of course), pretty short legs (as all Welsh corgis should have, as we are "herders" and just the right height to nip at the heels of the sheep), a pretty short tail (actually not much tail at all—not in the Pembroke breed), and a pretty nice life. Sometimes I feel they should have called me "Fred." You know how everybody makes fun of the name "Fred"? In the movies Fred is always the goofus . . . "Freds" are usually "flippin' the burgers," "fillin' her up" . . . you name it. When there's a Fred around, the eyeballs are rollin' and the laughin' begins . . . sometimes I hurt, like "Freds" must feel when joked about.

I am the new kid on the block (alias, "S.O.B") . . . arrived in Charleston last January . . . one of the "Northerners" they like to write about in the *Post & Courier* and say are "moving in" and chasing all the nice young families out of the Battery. . . . Well, as soon as I got here, the routines started. Early each morning, I would get all hooked up with that pretty purple leash, and would have to go "jogging"—we were in training for the Bridge Run of course. Well, I don't particularly *like* jogging . . . maybe it is because of these pretty short legs. Whatever the reason, it is okay, because I would rather get tied up at the market for an hour or so and socialize with the straw-basket ladies. That became the routine. Then Mama would continue to jog and leave me tied to the bench at the marketplace to be laughed at. So many people seem to make fun of me. The ladies who got to know me were kind to me, but the passersby would laugh at my short pretty self and make fun of me and say things like, "Well, I guess she hasn't missed a meal for a while—any lower to the ground, she'd be the limbo queen." Then there are the horses and carriages. I usually spend my daytime hours lying by the black iron gate in front of my historic house and waiting for the horses to draw the carriages by. When I first arrived, the carriage tourists really didn't notice me much, but after about a month, the tour guide added a little blurb about *me* to his narratives. As the driver draws the carriage near the front of my house, it goes something like, "Oh, and that is Camilla . . . she is a descendant of the Queen of England and has just moved here from Boston. She probably arrived on the Mayflower . . . and, as you can see, she will not be getting anywhere too quickly with those little short legs. Looks like maybe she's gotten knocked up with that big belly!" Everybody roars with laughter! Much funnier than talking about architecture, I guess.

While I am *not* pregnant, I *am* of Mayflower descent and I love Charleston. And I want Charleston to love me, to call me Camilla, and not treat me like a Fred!

CAMILLA

200

SERA

Ever wonder why man's best friend is a dog? Think about it. Dogs are blindly loyal. They are happy to see him no matter where he's been or how he smells. They don't interrogate man after a hard day at work. And never, ever would suggest he stop and ask directions.

But if I were a dog, I would want to be a woman's best friend. A single woman would be best. All that pent-up emotion and affection that men deflect goes to the dogs. And there is lots of it.

I knew I was in trouble when I started referring to my dog as my significant other. But that is the best way to describe Sera. We've been sharing a bed for seven years, so it's more than a casual relationship. We eat, sleep, and play together. We vacation together. My friends inquire about Sera as if she were a human counterpart. My friends relate to her as one of our peer group.

My closest friends are single women. Each is deeply involved in a relationship with a dog. We talk about our loved ones just like married couples do. "I have to get home. Sera hasn't had dinner yet." "Did you see the sunset? Sera and I were watching it together." "Sera's snoring woke me and I couldn't get back to sleep."

My mother accepts Sera as her grandchild. She spoils Sera as she did the other kids. And Sera plays Mom like a pro. The family was vacationing at our beach house. As we were moving in, my brother-in-law expressed concern about Sera getting along with his family cat, Charlie. Charlie immediately found a bed to hide under and watched from there. My sister and the kids were bringing in suitcases and groceries. Mom was in the kitchen putting away the food with Sera supervising. As Mom moved, so did Sera, her big brown eyes hungrily watching every package that passed overhead. An easy mark, Mom was feeding Sera a taste-of-this, a taste-of-that. After about an hour, we led Sera out of the kitchen to introduce her to her cat cousin. Just as cat and dog were about to check each other out, Mom rustled something in the kitchen and Sera took off to see what she was missing. Charlie went back under the bed.

A woman's relationship with her dog is intense. Linda called me long distance in tears. "Macho bit me. I can't believe he would turn on me like that." Macho is a Yorkie with a temper. It wasn't a nasty bite. Mostly it was the horror of having your best friend bite the hand that feeds him. It was reminiscent of all the men who had betrayed her. They considered counseling.

When is a dog not a dog? When a dog becomes a woman's best friend. I opened my heart and my home to Sera. In return, she is always there for me. She watches what I eat, but has never commented on my weight gain. She never criticizes my attire. When I feel bad, she sticks to me like a bandage. It's a relationship more valuable than the Hope Diamond. So what if she's a dog. She is my best friend.

LES SCHWARTZ

HIGGINS

There I had found myself. Cold, alone, and lonely. Crammed into a ten-by-ten-foot kennel run with five other big dogs. I had way too much energy to be crammed in there with no room to run or play. It was a constant fight for food, on the days we were fed. We had very little water. The kennel was rarely cleaned, so we had to walk in our own messes. I hated it there. I was alone, afraid, and scared.

I had come from a shelter in Florida all the way to Maryland. This place was supposed to be a "rescue." But I didn't feel "rescued." At least at the shelter I always had something to eat. At the Maryland kennel I was hungry, lonely, cramped. I didn't fight with the other dogs for food, so I stayed thin. I didn't want to get in their way and cause a potential fight, so I started turning in circles to get out some of my excess energy.

All I could think about was the place I had stayed on the way up to Maryland. It was such a long trip that the cats and I who were coming to the rescue kennel had to stop overnight in South Carolina. A nice lady, her husband, and their little boy agreed to let us stay with them. It was such a beautiful place. Not much when viewed by people standards probably, but to a dog who had spent his whole one year of life in a shelter, it was *heaven*! Of course I was scared to death. I was used to being in a shelter where I was lucky to get a pat on the head once a day. But when I saw that green yard all fenced in, and when the nice lady let me off the leash, I was so happy! I just ran and ran and ran. The nice lady brought out food. There was plenty of clean water to drink. And there were even other dogs to play with. I wasn't sure what to make of it, so I kind'a hung in the shadows that night.

That night I prayed that I would get to stay in this heavenly place. But, unfortunately, the next morning the lady and her husband cornered me in the yard and put the leash back on me. The nice lady told me not to be afraid. She said that I was going to go to a place where they would find me a good home. I didn't know what was wrong with this one, but what choice did I have?

So that is how I ended up at the "rescue." Cramped, hungry, thirsty, and alone, spinning in endless circles just to keep from going completely bonkers.

One day the people from animal control got wind of how all of us were being treated at this "rescue." They came in and took us all to the shelter. A shelter was not nearly as nice as that one night of heaven in South Carolina, but at least I got fed there. I was happy to eat and drink, and I slept well that night. But I couldn't forget about the nice lady with the big green yard.

It just so happens that all that praying was working its miracle. A very concerned woman on the board at the shelter sent an e-mail to all of the people who had helped get those animals to what they thought was "safety." She received a frantic e-mail back from a lady in South Carolina asking about a red dog named "Higgins."

Well, the lady in Maryland did not know my name. She didn't know any of the names of the dogs that were in the "rescue." But she started sending digital photos via e-mail to the lady in South Carolina. Finally one of the photos was me.

The lady in South Carolina said that she wanted to adopt me. But the rest of the women on the board at the shelter did not want to do that. They wanted to have me put to sleep. They said I was too shy and scared to ever fit into a family life. They said that this woman in South Carolina already had too many dogs, and a young child.

But the woman from South Carolina kept on asking. She sent in letters of reference from veterinarians, coworkers, friends, and family. And the first lady on the board kept trying to help me too. Finally a trainer was called in. She said I had no "fear aggression" at all (whatever that means). To me it simply meant that I would finally get to go back to heaven in South Carolina.

So the lady and her friend drove all the way from South Carolina to Maryland just to get me. I was scared when she first came into my run at the shelter. But she just lay on the ground and put a treat on the ground next to her. I had never seen a person act this way before.

Eventually I let her put a leash and harness on me, and we took the long drive back to heaven. When we got there, she took me into the house. I had never been in a house before, but it was nice and warm. I stayed very close to the nice lady, as she was the only thing I knew in this place.

The next morning she took me out to the big green yard. She took me off of my leash. I wanted to please her, so I walked into one of the open kennels and waited for her to close the door. But, to my surprise, she said,

"No, Higgins, no more kennels for you." I looked around. I looked both ways. She was serious. My face lit up and I began to run. I ran and ran and ran. I ran around that acre for at least an hour until I collapsed with pleasure, panting and smiling from ear to ear. I was finally home.

And that nice lady is now my mama. My mama wasn't lying to me that day. I have never been in a kennel since. That was over one year ago. I am free and happy, and I have a huge family to love me. Not bad for a shelter dog, hey?

HIGGINS

PIEBALD
("PIE-B")

A much loved black-and-white (party colored) cocker spaniel. Born with a congenital eye disease, he lived to four happy years. Piebald liked to sing and to chew bubble gum.

When voice lessons were practiced, he was shooed away. Only to hide around the sliding doors to get his two cents in.

Lying down, he took the balled pre-chewed gum between his front paws, pulled it with his mouth as far back as his head would go, and then wiggle-waggle the strung-out gum with his mouth back down to his paws in a tidy ball. Then to do over again!

He was much missed, our Pie-B.

P.S. Piebald liked to find the peanut butter sandwich crusts and hide them in the coal bucket for midnight snacks.

LIZZY

I grew up in a household where dogs "were kept outside." So, while I had animals, I never had pets. Five years ago I was at one of my son's ball games, and I happened to look around and see this couple carrying two little, beautiful, black balls of fur. I couldn't resist and asked if I could hold one. Well, that was all it took! I fell in love for the first time with an animal. This little creature cuddled up next to my chest and slept for the entire game. My son started yelling from the field asking if he could keep her. Since I had never had an inside dog, I had qualms. I knew exactly who would be taking care of her—me. Finally, after much trepidation, I agreed to take her home with promises from my eleven-year-old son that he would do all the work. Ha! From day one Lizzy was my dog. (For some reason my son, Jake, decided to call her "Lizzy" because of a little girl named "Lizzy" whom he didn't like. Remember, he was only eleven.)

Lizzy knew I was smitten, and she quickly took over the house. She was supposed to be a chow, but the only things "chow" were her black tongue and the frizzy hair on her ears. During the first visit to the vet, I learned that she was "mixed"—in other words, a "Heinz-57," for those of us raised in the South. I also learned that puppies are just like babies. They cry and have to go to the bathroom at all hours of the night. After the first couple of weeks of constantly cleaning the carpets, I was ready to pull my hair out! I didn't know the first thing about the potty-training of a mutt. I was moaning one day, and a friend suggested that I "kennel" her—Lizzy, that is. I thought that she meant for me to send her away.

After "kenneled" was explained to me, I went shopping and paid sixty dollars for a cage! This actually worked. Things were finally starting to look up. Originally one of the things that my son and I had talked about was how Lizzy would sleep in his room. Well, Lizzy decided that she needed a queen-size, four-poster bed to stretch out on. (Keep in mind, she already had decided that I was a wuss and that she ruled the household.) Plus, she decided that my room was much cleaner than Jake's, and she definitely didn't like his music. (Besides that, she could fit under my bed.) So Lizzy became my dog. She would follow me from room to room when I was home and start barking as soon as she saw my car pull in the driveway.

Speaking of barking, Lizzy barks at anything and everything. One day she saw a squirrel in the backyard and got so excited that she put her paw through one of the window panes! Fortunately for her, the paw was fine. Five years later, at fifty pounds, Lizzy is still my dog, and she still sleeps on my bed, and she still gets excited when I drive up. (She gets excited when Jake comes home too, just not as much.) I always threaten her that she can't die before me because I need her too much. I've also decided that dogs are much easier to raise than teenagers. They don't talk back, they're rarely ever moody, every night they lick you on the arm or leg because they love you, and they never, ever, use up all the gas in your car.

ANN RAMSEY

SADIE

I would like for you to meet my furry friend Sadie. A little over two years ago the administrator of the nursing home where I work mentioned that a lady had called and wanted to know if we needed a dog for pet therapy. (I'm the activities director, and pet therapy is one of the activities we provide and one that the residents love.) Sadie was owned by an elderly couple, and the gentleman had passed away. The wife was moving in with the daughter, who already had dogs, and the vet thought Sadie would do well in a nursing-home setting. Sadie was dropped off, and it was "love at first sight" for most of us. (Sadie wasn't too sure about us at the beginning, but she adjusted quickly.) Sadie was beautiful. She had long black hair, with lots of gray (she was twelve years old), had big gentle eyes, and walked on three legs. She had lost the other leg in an accident as a puppy, but being an amputee didn't stop Sadie. She quickly began to know her way around the nursing home and the various rooms where she "knew" which residents needed a visit. Very quickly she also became acquainted with which staff offices had doggy treats.

I had the good fortune to take Sadie home with me

one weekend to visit. My dog Lizzy was totally rude and thought that her position in my household had been usurped. Sadie was very gracious and just took everything in stride. But by the end of the weekend Lizzy was starting to come around, especially on Monday morning when I put Sadie in my car to return to work. Sadie eventually made her home with Heather, one of our occupational therapists. Heather would bring her in during the day and take her back home at night.

Sadie was gentle and loving with the residents and loved to roll over in the hallway, play dead, and hope that someone would stop and pet her, which almost always happened.

Sadie also had an outside job. She would often go with Heather to "amputee meetings" and show "humans" who had lost limbs what you could accomplish when you put your mind to it. She especially was a strong inspiration to a young man in his twenties who was a new amputee.

Unfortunately, during the last few months Sadie has started to slow down. She now has severe joint problems in her two good back legs and often has to be carried. We know eventually that Sadie will have to be put to sleep, and this breaks our hearts. Sadie has brought so much joy to our residents and staff, especially Heather and me. But I also know how much fun Sadie is going to have when she gets to that special garden in heaven set aside for our pets and realizes that she now has four legs to get around on. She might even be able to finally catch one of "those squirrels." We love you, Sadie.

ANN RAMSEY

Jiggs Campbell ("Lovebug," "Cutie," "Mr. Jiggs")

I was born weird—at least that's what I've been told. And that's why my mommy named me "Jiggs." She thinks that I act strange and that I have a weird ear. My predecessor, also a miniature schnauzer, was very well mannered. He waited to be invited to come in, and he liked to sleep in the grass. On the other hand, I see no sense in being invited anywhere. If I want to go in, I run in; and if I want to get on the furniture, I jump right up on the furniture. I don't like to lie in the grass; I like to eat the grass.

As a puppy I took great pleasure in making confetti. I made it out of newspapers, telephone books, books, maps, straw hats. I could fool people into thinking a tornado had blown through a room. It was always a challenge to do my work when no one was looking, but it was a challenge at which I was wildly successful.

I became a Charleston dog only recently. I spent my first two years in Columbia and had a very large yard on a lake. I could roam at will and leave deposits wherever I pleased, because we had lots and lots of bushes, trees, and pinestraw. One of the main changes

I've encountered in Charleston is that my yard is small. This presents a problem. My mommy always takes me on walks, and whenever I try to lay claim to some space, she snatches it up in a bag. I find this quite perplexing.

Another big difference is that people are always walking past our house. That kinda bugs me because I always thought people who come to the house are coming *into the house*. So I bark. I bark because it makes me so excited. I get excited because everyone who comes to our house is a playmate. I meet them all with one of my toys and try to make them chase me. Often, though, my mommy makes them do stuff like hang mirrors or crawl under the house. Then they leave, and I don't blame them. My favorite visitor is Brad. He always chases me, hides, and plays with me for a long time. My mommy is pretty good too. We play mostly at night. She chases me around the dining room table and all through the house. She turns off all the lights and waits for me to look for her. When I get near her, she screams and it makes me wilder.

The picture you see is of me and my duck, my favorite toy. My other favorite toy is a lamb with two squeakers. I always make lots of noise with it when people are talking. Then they try to grab it and throw it. It makes a great chase game.

I do love Charleston. Every time we go walking, we see lots of other dogs. My two best friends are Maude and Harold. They look like twins, and people always talk about how cute they are. My mommy says that I'm cute too and that's why she calls me "Cutie." It's funny how people who don't know me know my nickname because they frequently greet me with, "Hi, Cutie!" I guess I'm getting pretty well known around here.

JIGGS

KATIE SCARLETT

Katie Scarlett came to Pet Helpers Rescue & Adoption Shelter on James Island from the Mt. Pleasant Animal Control Center. Named "Katie Scarlett" after her Southern roots and all-black coat, she was automatically a shelter favorite. (They all are.)

As a resident of Pet Helpers, Katie Scarlett did not let being labeled "adoptable" get to her. She probably thought as did Scarlett O'Hara in *Gone with the Wind:* "As God is my witness, as God is my witness they're not going to lick me. I'm going to live through this." And so she did as a spokespet for the private, nonprofit rescue and adoption shelter.

Katie Scarlett made two radio appearances on the Bridge at 105.5 and on Kirkman Broadcasting station's REAL Talk Radio 1340. Everyone cooed over her and claimed her as one of the cutest Bassadors (half Labrador and half basset hound) they had ever seen. And as an attractive unspayed female, she got plenty of offers from the unneutered male community, but refused them by saying, "Sir, you are no gentleman . . . I don't create unwanted litters."

Katie Scarlett also would have stood duty as Pet Helpers' spokespet on the local news during a live telethon asking callers to make donations, but she was scheduled at Dr. Bob Carleson's Veterinary Clinic to become a responsibly spayed lady that day.

All homeless, abused, and abandoned pets that are taken in at Pet Helpers Rescue & Adoption Shelter are provided with a safe, loving environment until they are adopted. They are all given medical care, which includes updating their shots, the spaying or neutering of them, and the implant of a microchip before they are adopted.

Katie Scarlett spent more time at Pet Helpers than the staff anticipated. Dogs, cats, rabbits, young and old, came and left the shelter with good families as Katie Scarlett watched them come and go and thought as Scarlett did in *Gone with the Wind:* "My life is over. Nothing will ever happen to me again." But it was not the right time for Katie Scarlett. The right family had to come along, and in Katie Scarlett's case they came from off just to find her.

A couple moving from San Diego to Charleston flew south to put a contract on their house. While visiting the city they decided to do some sightseeing, and as animal lovers they stopped by to visit the pets of Pet Helpers. They saw Katie Scarlett and immediately fell in love, saying that her personality reminded them so much of their basset hound–Labrador mix named Beaufort and that they could not leave. Upon visiting the dog several times throughout their trip, the couple became attached, but knew that they could not transport Katie Scarlett back and forth throughout their move East.

Knowing that Katie Scarlett was meant to be the addition to the couple's family that they had been looking for, they did not leave the state until Katie Scarlett was officially their pet. The couple preadopted Katie Scarlett, gave a donation to Pet Helpers for helping them find her, and even decided to board her until they got their belongings moved to Charleston. While it seemed that she waited a lifetime (eight months actually), all Katie Scarlett could think was: "Home. I'll go home. After all, tomorrow is another day."

ROBIN GREEN

RHETT

Through a friend of a friend the yellow Lab puppy was brought to me as a Christmas present in 1984. As a bachelor and a carriage driver in Historic Charleston, I was well suited for such a companion. Rhett was immediately welcomed into my family and quickly became a favorite. After growing up in a USAF active duty family with dachshunds and schnauzers, I had wanted a "big dog" all of my life.

In 1989 Rhett started "work" full time at Olde Towne Carriage Company at 20 Anson Street. He was five years old and very streetwise. He had been around horses and mules all of his life and came to accept them as fellow animals to be respected. His normal workday was about ten hours, which consisted of socializing with fellow employees, locals, and tourists, and then forcing a staff member to throw one of the rubber balls that we made the horse-urine markers out of. He was a retriever of the best order!

Whenever a minor scrape or injury occurred, I would take him to our friendly neighborhood veterinarian, Cynthia P. Smith. Dr. Smith would patch him up and send him back to the barn. If additional medication was required, she would tape the bottle to his collar and off he went. It was really handy being twenty feet away. The staff was always amicable and professional.

Rhett had a radius of about two blocks, in and around the city market. Several times he would get into "friendly" trouble. Once one of the city's Animal Control officers came by with a complaint. Apparently a tourist had purchased a hot dog from a street vendor only to have it "stolen" by a "very friendly yellow Lab" that promptly ran off toward the horse barns. I assured the officer that it couldn't be my dog. Just then Rhett came walking into the barn licking yellow mustard from around his mouth! We had a good laugh, and I offered to buy the visitor another treat. A stem warning kept the dog close to the barn for a few days.

On one of our many beautiful days, our friends at some local restaurants would call and say that Rhett was enjoying the generosity of their patrons while the floor-length windows to the establishments were open. He would end up satisfied and walk back to the barn.

Once, at the corner of North Market and Church streets, a new hotel dedication was being held. Everyone was there—the owners, local businessmen, dignitaries. Plus it was catered. Rhett was there too. It was hilarious to watch as he made his way through the impressive crowd.

He had his brushes with fame too. We lived on Society Street, so we did everything downtown. We met Mikhail Baryshnikov at the Gaillard Municipal Auditorium. We were playing Frisbee on the lawn in front when he arrived in a limousine to rehearse for a Spoleto event. I had thrown the Frisbee in the direction of the car, and when the great dancer got out, Rhett made a fantastic catch. Baryshnikov remarked, "What a great dog," and went on into the building.

Rhett met the members of the rock group The Black Crowes when we were walking late one night down George Street. His nose went into the air, and he ran around the auditorium toward Alexander Street. I caught up with him only to discover that he was attending an impromptu cookout at their tour bus after their evening show. The band was enjoying hot dogs and beverages while packing their gear. We met Chris Robinson, the lead singer, and several other members.

As a carriage operator, we were hired to provide carriage services for the entertainment industry. Rhett and I worked on a fashion shoot outdoors for *Vogue* magazine at the United States Customs House, at the corner of South Market and East Bay streets. Cindy Crawford was the model, and they needed a horse and carriage for background. We were required to be "on set" very early in the moming. The caterers provided a wonderful breakfast spread, and we enjoyed a nice visit with the beautiful Miss Crawford.

I was hired as a wrangler for the television movie *Scarlett*. The film was the sequel to the great movie *Gone with the Wind*. During the work we met several of the fine actors, including Timothy Dalton, who played the part of Rhett Butler.

Folks just passing by the barn were welcomed by Rhett too. He met Academy Award winner Robert Duvall, as well as Dennis Hopper, Kyra Sedgwick, Kirstie Alley, and Shelley Duvall—all of whom passed by, but not without a friendly nudge from Rhett.

Rhett was friendly to locals too. I like to think he left his "mark" everywhere. There is a stretch of sidewalk on Pinckney Street that he accidentally walked through after it had been poured and the workers had left.

He had his adventures elsewhere too. On Capers Island a friend threw a stick far into a pond on the island. Before I could say no, Rhett leapt off of the causeway and into the water after the stick. The gators sunning themselves on a mud flat went into the water. I thought Rhett was a goner. We all screamed and yelled for him to return, but he bad to retrieve that stick. He fetched his prize, walked onto the mud flat, shook the water off, turned, and swam back to us. Those gators were less than ten feet away from him, but they just watched. He climbed out and looked none the worse for wear.

He traveled everywhere with me, and when it was time to "mount up" in the truck cab, he wouldn't hesitate. A ride in the truck or the boat meant adventure, and he was up for it.

At age thirteen and a half he was done. When that time came to make the decision, Dr. Doug Berger helped me do the right thing. I'm grateful to this day. Rhett was a great dog and a better companion. After his passing, a friend asked me to take care of his black Lab, Ashley. He was in the United States Navy, and was to be deployed for a year. Ashley immediately went to "work" at the carriage company and continued the fine tradition set forth by Rhett.

Ashley was a fantastic dog and eventually moved to California. Bruck was the next big dog to take the reins. Labrador retrievers are great dogs, and I must admit, I can't live without them.

I have been blessed with great canine companionship, and thanks to some fine local veterinarians, the Labs' lives have been made better.

TONY YOUMANS

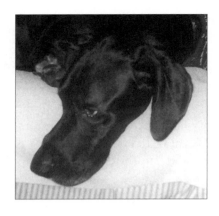

DRACULA

My name is Dracula. I'm a black, three-year-old, male Great Dane with a white bat on my chest (hence my name). My grandmother knew someone who was going to Myrtle Beach to pick up a three-month-old male Great Dane puppy, and he had a brother. She asked this person to pick me up also for a birthday present for her son sight unseen. Her son gave me my name. My brother lives downtown. He is larger than me and has a different personality.

When I was almost two years old, my grandmother's son moved to Pennsylvania with his girlfriend and I couldn't go. That's okay, because I've always lived with my grandmother and she loves me very much.

I have lots of friends at my grandma's. She has a rat terrier, Wheezer, who is fifteen years old and is the boss. I love playing with her, but she bites me when I get wild. Then there is Goliath, the black Labrador-pointer who belongs to my dad's brother, but he lives with Grandma also. I love to maul him. Goliath, Diamond, and I roughhouse all of the time.

Diamond is my other best friend. She is a red Pomeranian–chow chow, about twenty-five pounds. She thinks she is as big as us, and the three of us really love to play WWF smack down. We drag Diamond around by her neck or tail, and she bites our feet and legs. Silver, the beautiful blue merle tricolor prissy sheltie, plays some, but usually bites us for being so rowdy. Now Grandma has twin Pomeranians, Sassy and Foxy, who love to get right in my face and lick me all the time. They steal my bones and rawhides. I know that they love me, but sometimes they get on my nerves—always wanting to give me kisses. Silver likes to play as well, but it usually doesn't last long. She will let you know when she is done, let me tell ya!

We love to get in the van and go for rides, especially downtown. We get to walk through the market, and we get a lot of attention. I love the attention! Especially from the ladies. I also like little kids with food. They are the right height to give kisses.

The newest member of our family is a little male, tan-black, Chihuahua puppy named Valentino. Everyone calls him "Little Man." He thinks he is very macho. He enjoys getting on me and licking my ears and face. He always wants to be close to me. I growl at him, but he doesn't care. For such a diversified family, we all get along very well.

DRACULA

DIAMOND

Hi! My name is Diamond. I'm a female red Pomeranian–chow chow. I weigh almost twenty-seven pounds, but I think that I am a hundred pounds of attitude. I came from a lady who worked with my owner's daughter-in-law. She had my mom, and I was one of the puppies that didn't find a home. I was kept in a kennel on the porch and only came out to walk on a leash to use the bathroom. Every once in a while the neighborhood kids would let me out to play.

Then I went to my new home. I've been here about two years. I'm so happy with my new adopted brothers. We are fondly called the "gruesome threesome" by our family. Dracula is the biggest. The other part of our threesome is Goliath. We like to pull each others' tails and grab feet and legs. The three of us play very rough. Whoever goes out the door first waits for the other two in order to bite them. We love to race around the yard. I guess you could say we are like the three stooges.

In the summertime we get to have a large kids' pool filled with water and toys. Dracula will just stand in it to cool off. Goliath loves to go snorkling for the toys that sink, and he lies in the water to cool off. On the other hand, I love to lie on my side in the water and pull myself around the pool as fast as I can. I enjoy making the water swirl fast. Then I run around the yard soaking wet, collecting all the dirt I can, and then I jump back in the pool.

When our mom takes us downtown to walk in the market and to eat at Bubba Gumps, we get to wear our yellow reflector vest and our Outward Hound backpacks. My backpack is as big as Dracula's and Goliath's, but I don't care. It makes me one of the big dogs. I enjoy wearing my backpack and carrying things for Mom. I get upset when they try to take it off. I'm so short that my backpack almost touches the ground. At Bubba Gumps we sit out on the patio. The waitress brings us water with a lemon on the side and a small dish of ice cream.

Our mom bought a new van that is easier for us to get in and out of so we can go for rides. There is enough room for all of us to have a place to sit. We all love road trips. We each have our own dog kennel that we sleep in at night and when Mom is at work. She fixes up those rubber kongs with treats and smooth peanut butter, and freezes them. We have a favorite toy, our kong, and a fluffy dog bed in our kennels. We sleep until Mom comes home. On weekends we sometimes get to sleep in bed with Mom. We enjoy that very much.

I think that I was very lucky to find such a good family that wanted me. I wish all dogs could have a good home.

DIAMOND

FOXY AND SASSY

Hey! Our names are Foxy and Sassy. We are twin Pomeranians, apricot in color, and one year old. Our mother's name is Vickie. She loves all animals, and we think we have the biggest piece of her heart.

We remember the day Vickie and her oldest son, Joseph, came to see us. They were looking for only one puppy. Vickie's rat terrier, Wheezer, who was fourteen years old at the time, was in kidney failure, and Vickie was very attached to her. The lady who was selling us had bought us for her husband, who was very sick. They lived in a trailer park with a dirt yard. The lady said she wanted us to go together. We had to leave together on a chain. Vickie only wanted one of us—me, Foxy. Joseph said, "Mom, you can't leave one, you have to take both." So she did.

We settled in our new home pretty quick. We live with Dracula, Goliath, Wheezer, Silver, and Diamond. We also have cats, a rabbit, a cockatoo, and fish. We have a big backyard to run in, and Mom takes us a lot of places with her. We all love to ride in the van.

Our mom tells us we act like human twins. We think the same and act like bookends. Everyone, including

Mom once in a while, has trouble telling us apart.

Sassy and I had been living with Mom for about two months when Sassy jumped off of Dracula's crate. She broke her left leg. She had to wear a splint for ten weeks for it to heal. Sassy's legs are so little that the splint would slide off in her sleep. I slept with Mom all of the time, but when Sassy broke her leg she had to start sleeping with Mom also. Mom is a very light sleeper, and she would wake up every time Sassy would start chewing on the splint. Mom and Sassy became very close. Sassy acts like Wheezer does with Mom—they won't let Mom out of their sight. I'm the independent one. The same week that Sassy got her splint off of her broken leg with a two-inch laceration on it, she had to have sutures. Needless to say, she learned to walk on her back legs, and I copied her.

We both love to dress up in clothes and wear sunglasses. We get a lot of attention when we go places with Mom. Wheezer goes everywhere with us, and we have learned to act a lot like her. We all are very protective of Mom and do not like to share her. Sassy is the worst when another dog gets near Mom. Sassy looks like a rabid piranha.

Sassy and I sure love our new life with our mom.

FOXY

HAZEL AND SHILOH

Hello, my name is Hazel. I am eight years old in people years. I am a beautiful and petite (at my heaviest, thirty pounds) Boykin spaniel. Of course you know that the Boykin spaniel is the South Carolina dog. I have learned that fact from the many horse carriage guides who point me out to the tourists as I run by with my mother. Also, I would like to tell you about my good old friend who just passed away last December. His name was Shiloh. Shiloh was fourteen. He was the most beautiful and handsome yellow English Lab that you have ever seen. What a guy!

Shiloh and I met when I was just a puppy. Our parents had just started dating. We really hit it off, as did our parents. We would go on great walks together all over downtown Charleston. What a great city! There is always a park to play ball, and I love the Battery. I have even jumped the wall next to the Missroon House to take a swim on the small beach below. I really terrified my mother. She had to climb down and lift me back over the wall to a tourist nearby. Also, to all you ball lovers out there—there is always an ample supply of tennis balls around the tennis courts of Moultrie Playground. I cannot believe people forget to take their balls with them. I would never!

Back to Shiloh. My family and I have Shiloh to thank for helping my parents tie the knot. My mom arrived at my dad's house thinking that she was just going on a dinner date. Shiloh was all dressed up in his fancy, velvet, black, bow-tie collar. Hanging from the collar was a beautiful ice blue Tiffany jewelry bag and a note. My mother still had no clue what was actually happening! My dad said to read the note from Shiloh first. This is what it said: "My dad wants to know if you will marry him. Hazel and I have discussed it, and we think it is a good idea. Love, Shiloh." Wow! My mom was speechless. She just stood there. Finally my dad had to say, "Well, will you?" Thank goodness, she said yes! She even forgot to open the ring after all of the excitement. Of course she loved it too. Shiloh and I were thrilled!

Shiloh and I were very spoiled before the kids came into the picture. We both had great big beds in our parents' room, and even were allowed special time on the sofas to watch a movie or sports with Dad. We spent weekends at Wadmalaw Island and Sullivan's Island with our parents and grandparents. What a life! My favorite activity in the world is to play ball on the dock at Wadmalaw. I really don't even need a partner. I throw the ball off the high dock, run to the floating dock, jump in the water, retrieve the ball, and climb up the ladder to do this all over again. It is delightful. Shiloh loved to swim gracefully around the saltwater ponds. It kept him cool, and he was able to touch the bottom. I really miss Shiloh.

Shiloh passed away December 10, 2004. I have never seen my family, especially my dad, so upset. We all miss him. The children still call for "Shi Shi." There will never be another Lab as great as Shi.

I hope that I have told you a little bit about my life and my family. I am so lucky to be Hazel. I am loved and adored by my parents, grandparents, and now, sister and brother. Thank you.

Love,

HAZEL

ROCKEM SOCKEM ROO

Hello there! My name is Rockem Sockem Roo, but just plain Rocco does the trick . . . well, most of the time. I live with my mom Trish out on James Island, and I have become quite accustomed to my way of life in this fabulous city.

Now, I am originally from Texas, but please don't hold that against me because my mom brought me to Charleston just as soon as she could get her hands on me. She drove twenty hours to come pick me up, so I had to get used to long car rides pretty quickly. It was a good thing too because my mom and I drive all over the Charleston area to do fun things together. We make frequent visits to James Island Dog Park, and it's a good time for me to catch up and play with all of my friends. But I have a little too much fun there, and never want to come home when Mom says it's time to go. But she has learned this magic word, "treat," which can have me running to her in about two seconds flat. She has me completely figured out already.

My favorite part of Charleston though would have to

be Folly Beach. Despite my small size, my mom tells me I suffer from "Big-Dog Syndrome," which means I immediately take off full speed into the surf to play catch and roll around with all the other "Big Dogs." When she first took me to Folly Beach, she didn't realize that they never taught me how to swim in Texas, so she just threw me in the water. I was terrified at first and kept running back to the land, but with her help I caught on very quickly, and now she has to fight to keep me out of the water. She has given me yet another nickname of her own: "Little River Rat."

My mom got me during a rough time in her life, and I think that is the reason we are so close. I am sure that I am the only other being on the planet that can make her scold, cry, and laugh at me all within a span of about two minutes. But I know she loves me very much because she always smiles when I am around and she even lets me sleep in the bed with her. I make sure that she starts every day with a big lick on the face from me, and in return, I get a good rubdown and playtime. I love living in Charleston with my mom, and I am very excited because she assures me that we will be living here for a very long time.

ROCCO

[Photograph courtesy of Lese Corrigan]

ZOEY

Like Sadie Greenberg I am not really a Charleston Dog. In fact, I think I've never been to Charleston. But one of my adopters, a.k.a. "Alpha Bob," has been working on getting this book ready for the printer, and I've been right behind him the entire time. So I have found out quite a bit about you lucky dogs who live in Charleston. When they were living in Savannah, Alpha Bob and Alpha Karen visited Charleston, and they assure me that it is a beautiful city. (I'm "Alpha Dog," and my friend Zuni, who drops in often, is "Alpha Cat.")

I was described to my new family as a "Cock-a-Poo," but I think that I am much more eclectic than just a mixture of cocker spaniel and poodle. I do believe that there is a bit of terrier mixed in there. This is good since my much-loved predecessor was a mixed terrier (see *Savannah Dogs*, page 344). I don't mind when my new pack talk about Sarah, since there are plenty of compliments for both of us.

I was interested to see how many of you were also

"previous owner" dogs, and the different experiences you had. I myself was a "stray" (an episode I do not like to dwell on) and was picked up by Animal Control. They treated me very nicely, treats even, but the big dogs there were so noisy they scared me. I much preferred the "cat room" they had. I don't bark, so it was much more congenial. Well, I do bark, but only in my sleep, and then more of a "puppy yelp."

I've been in my new home about a month now, and am settling in quite nicely, but it does take a lot of time to train my new housemates. They never had a dog who liked to share their bed at night. This makes it hard to convince them of the fact that I get seventy-five percent of the space, while they are allowed a generous twenty-five percent, but they're learning.

I think that one of the things that impressed me most about the stories in this book is the heavy dependence on the word "love." I checked, and there are over one hundred and thirty uses of the word, about one per page. This compares to the thirty-three times that "food" appears. I think this is a significant indication of perhaps the most important contribution that we dogs provide for the world.

I want to thank the publishers of this book for allowing me to stick my paw into this fascinating collection of experiences.

ZOEY